Racing Pigeons Mastery Unleashed

The Ultimate Guide to Raising, Training, and Winning with Champion Birds

Kacy M. Drozd

Racing Pigeons Mastery Unleashed

Racing Pigeons Mastery Unleashed

TABLE OF CONTENTS

Racing Pigeons Mastery Unleashed

INTRODUCTION

In the quiet countryside of Belgium, a young farmer named Louis released his prized pigeon, a sleek bird named Éclair, into the crisp morning air. The race that day would cover over 500 miles, testing Éclair's endurance, speed, and unerring instinct to find his way home. As Louis watched Éclair disappear into the horizon, he felt a mixture of pride, hope, and nervous anticipation. Hours later, as the sun dipped low, a flutter of wings announced Éclair's return—his champion bird had bested hundreds of competitors to claim victory. This remarkable moment, repeated countless times across the globe, is at the heart of pigeon racing—a sport as ancient as it is thrilling.

Pigeon racing is not merely a competition; it is a testament to the bond between humans and these extraordinary birds. It combines the art of selective breeding, the science of training, and the thrill of competition. Whether you are a curious beginner or a seasoned racer, this book is your gateway into the fascinating world of racing pigeons.

Why Racing Pigeons?

Racing pigeons are remarkable creatures. Their unparalleled homing ability, combined with their speed and stamina, makes them true avian athletes. These birds possess a unique blend of instinct and intelligence, navigating vast distances to return to their lofts with incredible precision. For centuries, people have been captivated by their abilities, turning pigeon racing into a beloved sport that transcends borders, cultures, and generations.

But pigeon racing is more than a sport—it is a lifestyle. It requires patience, dedication, and an appreciation for the birds' innate talents. It is about building trust with your pigeons, understanding their needs, and pushing the boundaries of what they can achieve.

What You'll Learn in This Book

This comprehensive guide covers everything you need to know to excel in pigeon racing, from the basics to advanced strategies. Here's a glimpse of what lies ahead:

- **The Foundations of Racing Pigeons**: Discover the history and evolution of pigeon racing and the unique traits that make these birds exceptional competitors.

- **Building the Ideal Loft**: Learn how to create a safe, efficient, and comfortable home for your pigeons.

- **Training for Success**: Understand the step-by-step process of conditioning pigeons for races, including techniques to enhance their stamina, speed, and homing instincts.

- **Breeding Champions**: Explore the art and science of breeding pigeons for superior genetics, focusing on traits like endurance and agility.

- **Nutrition and Health**: Dive into the dietary needs of racing pigeons and strategies to keep them in peak physical condition.

- **Strategies for Winning**: Gain insights into race-day preparation, reading weather conditions, and leveraging advanced technology to track and analyze your birds' performance.

- **Community and Competitions**: Connect with the global pigeon racing community and learn how to participate in races, join clubs, and network with fellow enthusiasts.

For Beginners and Experts Alike

Whether you are taking your first steps into the world of pigeon racing or you are an experienced fancier seeking advanced tips, this book has been designed to meet your needs. Beginners will find clear explanations and step-by-step guides, while experts will appreciate the in-depth strategies and advanced techniques.

Why This Book Stands Out

This is more than just a how-to guide; it is a celebration of the sport and the birds that make it possible. Every chapter has been crafted with care to ensure it is informative, engaging, and actionable. The advice in these pages comes from seasoned pigeon fanciers, drawing on decades of experience to provide you with proven methods for success.

A Journey Worth Taking

The path of a pigeon racer is one of constant learning, adaptation, and triumph. It is about the quiet satisfaction of watching your pigeons take flight, the thrill of a well-earned victory, and the camaraderie of a community that shares your passion. By the end of this book, you will not only have the tools to succeed but also a deeper appreciation for the extraordinary partnership between humans and pigeons.

So, let's begin this journey together. Like Louis and his champion Éclair, you too can experience the joy of unleashing the potential of your racing pigeons—and perhaps even claim your own place among the greats of this timeless sport.

CHAPTER ONE

THE LEGACY OF PIGEON RACING

Pigeon racing is a sport steeped in history, combining the timeless bond between humans and pigeons with the excitement of competition. To truly appreciate the modern-day intricacies of this fascinating pursuit, it is essential to explore its roots, its global impact, and the pivotal role racing pigeons have played throughout history.

Origins of Pigeon Racing

The origins of pigeon racing can be traced back thousands of years to ancient civilizations that recognized the extraordinary homing abilities of these birds. In Egypt, pigeons were revered not only as messengers but also as symbols of loyalty and endurance. Similarly, the Greeks used pigeons to announce victories in the Olympic Games, a testament to their unmatched speed and reliability.

By the 19th century, pigeon racing had evolved into a structured sport, particularly in Belgium, where it gained immense popularity. Belgian fanciers meticulously bred pigeons for speed, stamina, and homing instincts, laying the foundation for modern racing standards. The passion for the sport quickly spread to neighboring countries and beyond, eventually reaching global prominence.

Today, pigeon racing is not merely a pastime but a respected sport with an international following. Its rich history continues to inspire new generations of enthusiasts, connecting them to a tradition that spans continents and centuries.

Global Appeal and Notable Achievements

Pigeon racing is celebrated worldwide, with dedicated fanciers in countries as diverse as Belgium, the United States, China, and South Africa. The sport's global appeal lies in its accessibility—anyone with a passion for pigeons and the commitment to train them can participate. This inclusivity has fostered a vibrant international community that shares techniques, stories, and a love for these remarkable birds.

One of the most notable achievements in pigeon racing history occurred in 2019, when a Belgian racing pigeon named *Armando* was sold for a record-breaking $1.4 million. Known as "the Lewis Hamilton of pigeons," Armando's success highlighted the extraordinary value placed on champion birds.

Another remarkable feat is the famous World War II hero pigeon, *Cher Ami*, who delivered a critical message that saved nearly 200 soldiers despite being gravely injured. Such stories underscore the incredible capabilities of pigeons and their profound impact on human endeavors.

The Role of Racing Pigeons in History

Beyond the racetrack, pigeons have played pivotal roles in human history, serving as messengers, war heroes, and symbols of hope. Their unmatched homing instinct and ability to navigate vast distances made them indispensable during times when communication technologies were limited.

During both World Wars, pigeons were enlisted as messengers, carrying crucial information across enemy lines. Their bravery and reliability earned many pigeons medals of honor, including the Dickin Medal, often referred to as the "animal Victoria Cross." These wartime contributions demonstrated not only the physical prowess of pigeons but also the deep trust humans placed in them.

Pigeons have also been used in peacekeeping efforts and scientific research. Their uncanny ability to find their way home has inspired studies on navigation, magnetism, and even avian intelligence.

The Legacy Lives On
The legacy of pigeon racing is a rich tapestry woven with history, culture, and human ingenuity. From ancient Egypt to modern global championships, racing pigeons have captivated generations with their extraordinary abilities and unwavering loyalty.

As you embark on your journey into the world of pigeon racing, remember that you are participating in a tradition that has stood the test of time. You are not just racing pigeons; you are celebrating a legacy that reflects the enduring bond between humans and these remarkable birds.

CHAPTER TWO

UNDERSTANDING RACING PIGEONS

Racing pigeons are remarkable creatures, uniquely equipped to excel in the demanding sport of competitive racing. They combine athletic prowess with an exceptional homing instinct, making them unparalleled among avian athletes. This chapter delves into the physical, scientific, and psychological aspects that define racing pigeons as champions of the skies.

Anatomy of a Champion

Racing pigeons owe their extraordinary speed and endurance to their finely tuned anatomy. Every part of their body is designed for efficient and powerful flight.

- **Streamlined Build**: Racing pigeons have slender, aerodynamic bodies that reduce drag during flight, allowing them to maintain high speeds for extended periods.

- **Powerful Wing Muscles**: Their well-developed wing muscles generate the strength needed for long-distance flights. These muscles account for about a third of their total body weight, emphasizing their importance in flight mechanics.

- **Efficient Respiratory System**: Racing pigeons possess a highly efficient respiratory system, complete with air sacs that store and circulate oxygen during flight. This ensures a constant supply of energy even during strenuous races.

- **Large Heart**: Their hearts are significantly larger, relative to body size, compared to most birds. This allows them to pump oxygen-rich blood efficiently, sustaining their physical output over long distances.

- **Sharp Vision**: With exceptional eyesight, pigeons can spot landmarks and environmental cues from great heights, aiding navigation and orientation during races.

These anatomical traits, honed through generations of selective breeding, make racing pigeons exceptional athletes.

The Science Behind the Homing Instinct

One of the most fascinating aspects of racing pigeons is their uncanny ability to find their way home, even from hundreds of miles away. This homing instinct has been the subject of extensive scientific study and remains a marvel of nature.

- **Environmental Landmarks**: Pigeons use visual cues such as rivers, mountains, and roads to navigate their route home. Their sharp vision helps them recognize these features from high altitudes.

- **Solar Compass**: Pigeons rely on the position of the sun to determine direction and adjust their course. They can even account for the sun's movement throughout the day, ensuring accurate navigation.

- **Magnetic Fields**: Research suggests that pigeons detect the Earth's magnetic field through specialized cells in their beaks. This natural compass helps them orient themselves during overcast days or unfamiliar routes.

- **Olfactory Cues**: Surprisingly, pigeons may also use their sense of smell to identify familiar odors near their home loft. This ability helps them fine-tune their approach as they near their destination.

The homing instinct is not just a biological phenomenon; it's also a skill that can be nurtured and strengthened through proper training and experience.

Psychological Traits for Racing Success

Beyond their physical attributes and natural instincts, racing pigeons possess a unique set of psychological traits that contribute to their racing prowess.

- **Intelligence**: Pigeons are highly intelligent birds capable of learning complex tasks. They quickly adapt to training routines, recognize patterns, and memorize routes.

- **Focus and Determination**: During a race, pigeons demonstrate incredible focus, staying on course despite distractions, weather challenges, or fatigue. Their singular goal is to return to their home loft as quickly as possible.

- **Adaptability**: Racing pigeons are remarkably adaptable, thriving in various environments and handling changes in weather or terrain with ease. This adaptability is crucial for success in competitive racing, where conditions are often unpredictable.

- **Bond with Their Loft**: The homing instinct is strongly tied to their sense of attachment to their home loft. This bond motivates pigeons to overcome challenges and fly tirelessly until they reach their destination.

By understanding these psychological traits, pigeon fanciers can develop effective training strategies that align with the natural behavior of their birds, enhancing their performance in races.

Racing pigeons are a blend of nature's brilliance and human ingenuity. Their exceptional anatomy, finely tuned homing instinct, and unique psychological traits make them a force to be reckoned with in the world of competitive racing. Understanding these characteristics is essential for anyone looking to succeed in the sport or appreciate the remarkable capabilities of these birds.

In the next chapter, we will explore the art of creating the ideal environment for racing pigeons, from designing efficient lofts to establishing routines that ensure their health, comfort, and performance.

CHAPTER THREE

SETTING UP FOR SUCCESS

Success in pigeon racing starts with a solid foundation. This chapter guides you through the essential steps for preparing your racing pigeons to excel, focusing on creating the right environment, equipping yourself with the proper tools, and selecting the best birds to begin your journey.

Designing the Ideal Loft

A well-designed loft is the cornerstone of any successful racing pigeon setup. It provides a safe, comfortable, and efficient space where your birds can thrive.

- **Location Matters**: Choose a location for your loft that offers good sunlight exposure and is away from potential predators or noisy disturbances. Elevation can also be beneficial, as it gives pigeons a clear flight path during training and races.

- **Ventilation**: Proper airflow is critical to maintaining the health of your pigeons. A well-ventilated loft helps reduce the risk of respiratory diseases, which are common in crowded or poorly ventilated environments. Adjustable vents and windows can help regulate airflow throughout the year.

- **Space and Layout**: A racing loft should be spacious enough to accommodate your pigeons without overcrowding. Each bird should have its own perch to avoid conflicts. Divide the loft into sections for nesting, training, and resting, ensuring an organized and stress-free environment.

- **Hygiene and Cleaning**: The loft should be easy to clean, with a floor design that allows for quick removal of droppings. Regular cleaning is essential to prevent disease and maintain a healthy living space.

- **Security**: Protect your pigeons from predators such as cats, hawks, and rodents. Use sturdy materials for the loft construction, and ensure all openings are properly sealed or fitted with wire mesh to keep unwanted visitors out.

A well-thought-out loft not only enhances the comfort of your pigeons but also lays the groundwork for their peak performance during training and racing.

Essential Tools and Equipment

Equipping your loft with the right tools ensures that your pigeons receive the best care and training. Here are the essentials every pigeon racer should have:

- **Perches and Nest Boxes**: Provide comfortable perches for your pigeons to rest on and nest boxes for breeding pairs. These should be designed to minimize stress and promote healthy behavior.

- **Feeders and Waterers**: Invest in durable feeders and waterers that are easy to clean and refill. Fresh water and high-quality feed are non-negotiable for maintaining your pigeons' health and energy levels.

- **Training Baskets**: Training baskets allow you to transport pigeons safely during training sessions and races. Choose lightweight but sturdy baskets that offer proper ventilation.

- **Health and Grooming Supplies**: Stock up on essentials such as vitamins, supplements, medications, and grooming tools to keep your pigeons in top condition.

- **Electronic Timing System (ETS)**: For competitive racing, an ETS is indispensable. These systems automatically record your pigeons' return times, providing accurate and efficient results.

- **Cleaning Tools**: Invest in scrapers, disinfectants, and brushes to maintain a clean loft and minimize the risk of disease.

- **Record-Keeping Tools**: A notebook, computer software, or dedicated app can help you track your pigeons' training, health, and racing performance over time.

Having the right equipment ensures you can manage your pigeons effectively and focus on their development without unnecessary distractions.

Selecting Your First Racing Pigeons
Choosing the right birds to start your loft is one of the most important decisions you'll make as a pigeon racer. Here's what to consider:

- **Proven Pedigrees**: Look for pigeons with a lineage of strong racers. Birds bred from successful racers often inherit traits such as speed, stamina, and a strong homing instinct.

- **Physical Characteristics**: Healthy pigeons typically have bright eyes, smooth feathers, and a strong, symmetrical body. Check for well-muscled chests and well-aligned wings, which are crucial for powerful flight.

- **Behavior and Temperament**: Choose birds that are alert, active, and confident. A calm yet focused demeanor often indicates a bird's ability to handle the stresses of racing.

- **Age Considerations**: Young pigeons are easier to train and bond with their loft, making them ideal for beginners. Older pigeons, however, may already have some training, which can be an advantage if they're accustomed to competitive racing.

- **Compatibility**: Ensure that the pigeons you select can coexist harmoniously in the loft. This minimizes conflicts and creates a positive environment for training and racing.

Starting with a small number of quality pigeons is better than overwhelming yourself with too many birds. As you gain experience, you can gradually expand your loft and refine your breeding and training strategies.

Setting up for success involves thoughtful planning and preparation. By designing a functional and comfortable loft, equipping it with the right tools, and selecting high-quality pigeons, you create the ideal environment for your birds to thrive and excel.

CHAPTER FOUR

NUTRITION FOR PEAK PERFORMANCE

Racing pigeons are elite athletes of the avian world, and like all athletes, their performance is directly tied to their diet. Proper nutrition is the foundation for endurance, speed, and overall health, making it one of the most critical aspects of pigeon care. This chapter delves into the fundamentals of pigeon nutrition, specialized diets for racing seasons, and the use of supplements and hydration strategies to ensure your birds perform at their peak.

Fundamentals of Pigeon Nutrition

A balanced diet is essential for maintaining the health, strength, and stamina of racing pigeons. Each nutrient plays a unique role in supporting the bird's body and mind, ensuring they are ready for the physical demands of training and racing.

- **Proteins**: Proteins are the building blocks for muscle repair and growth. Pigeons require high-quality protein sources such as peas, beans, and lentils, especially during molting and recovery periods.

- **Carbohydrates**: Carbs are the primary energy source for pigeons. Grains like corn, wheat, and barley provide the quick-release energy needed for intense flights.

- **Fats**: Healthy fats, such as those found in sunflower seeds and linseed, are crucial for sustained energy during long-distance races. Fats act as a reserve fuel source when carbohydrate stores are depleted.

- **Vitamins and Minerals**: Vitamins A, D, E, and B-complex support overall health, immunity, and energy metabolism. Minerals like calcium, phosphorus, and magnesium strengthen bones and regulate muscle function.

- **Fiber**: Small amounts of fiber aid digestion and maintain gut health, which is essential for nutrient absorption.

Understanding the roles of these nutrients helps pigeon racers design a diet that meets the specific needs of their birds, ensuring they remain in optimal condition year-round.

Special Diets for Racing Seasons

During the racing season, the nutritional demands of pigeons increase significantly. Crafting a racing-specific diet is key to maximizing their speed and endurance.

- **Pre-Race Nutrition**: A high-energy diet is essential in the days leading up to a race. Increase the proportion of carbohydrates, such as corn and rice, to provide the quick energy needed for flight. Avoid overloading on protein, as it can weigh birds down.

- **Post-Race Recovery**: After a race, the focus shifts to replenishing energy stores and repairing muscle tissue. Incorporate a mix of proteins and easily digestible carbohydrates, such as peas and soft grains, to aid recovery.

- **Seasonal Adjustments**: Modify the diet based on the racing calendar. During training, provide a balanced diet to build stamina, and introduce higher fat content for longer races to sustain energy over extended periods.

A well-planned diet tailored to the demands of racing ensures your pigeons are always prepared to perform their best, regardless of the competition's intensity.

Supplements and Hydration Strategies

In addition to a nutritious diet, supplements and proper hydration play a crucial role in enhancing a racing pigeon's stamina, health, and recovery.

- **Vitamins and Minerals**: Supplements like multivitamins can fill any nutritional gaps in the diet. Calcium and phosphorus are particularly important for strong bones and eggshell formation in breeding pigeons.

- **Electrolytes**: During races and hot weather, pigeons lose essential salts through sweat. Electrolyte supplements added to drinking water help maintain fluid balance, prevent dehydration, and reduce fatigue.

- **Probiotics**: Healthy gut bacteria support digestion and immunity. Probiotic supplements improve nutrient absorption, ensuring your pigeons get the most from their diet.

- **Amino Acids**: Amino acids like lysine and methionine aid in muscle repair and feather quality, which are essential for endurance and aerodynamics.

- **Hydration Tips**: Fresh, clean water must be available at all times. During training and races, consider offering water mixed with glucose or electrolytes to provide an immediate energy boost.

Proper hydration and supplementation give your pigeons the edge they need to recover faster, stay healthier, and perform consistently at their peak.

Nutrition is the secret weapon of every successful pigeon racer. By understanding the fundamentals of pigeon nutrition, implementing special diets for the racing season, and leveraging supplements and hydration strategies, you can unlock your pigeons' full potential.

CHAPTER FIVE

TRAINING THE ATHLETE

The process of transforming a young pigeon into a racing champion is both an art and a science. It requires patience, consistency, and a deep understanding of the bird's natural abilities and instincts. This chapter covers the foundational steps of training, progressively building physical endurance and mental sharpness to prepare your pigeons for the challenges of competitive racing.

Training Basics: From Loft to Short Flights

Every racing pigeon's journey begins in the loft, the heart of their training and home. Establishing trust and teaching homing skills are the initial building blocks of a successful training regimen.

- **Establishing Trust**: Building a bond with your pigeons is essential for effective training. Spend time in the loft, ensuring the birds are comfortable with your presence. Hand-feeding and gentle handling can foster trust and reduce stress.

- **Familiarizing Them with the Loft**: Before taking them outdoors, young pigeons must learn that the loft is their safe space. Allow them to explore it thoroughly and associate it with food, water, and comfort.

- **Short Flights Around the Loft**: Once they are familiar with the loft, begin by letting them take short flights around it. This step helps them develop spatial awareness and strengthens their wing muscles. Keep these sessions short initially, gradually increasing duration as their confidence grows.

- **Homing Skills**: After mastering local flights, start releasing them from short distances. Begin with a few hundred meters and gradually increase the range, always ensuring they have ample time to return before dark.

These foundational steps lay the groundwork for more advanced training, helping your pigeons build the confidence and homing skills needed for racing.

Progressive Distance Training

As your pigeons become comfortable with returning home from short distances, the focus shifts to building their endurance and speed. Progressive distance training systematically increases the challenge, conditioning the birds for long races.

- **Incremental Distance Increases**: Gradually extend the release point, moving from one kilometer to five, then ten, and eventually up to 50 kilometers or more. Each increase should be spaced out over days to avoid overexertion.

- **Varied Release Locations**: Changing release points helps prevent pigeons from becoming too dependent on specific landmarks. This ensures they rely more on their homing instincts and navigational skills.

- **Group and Individual Training**: While group releases simulate race conditions, occasional solo flights test each pigeon's individual skills and resilience. This balance ensures they can perform well in any scenario.

- **Early Morning Flights**: Training in the early morning mimics the conditions of many races, helping pigeons adjust to flying in cooler temperatures and dealing with dew-laden air.

Consistency is key in progressive training. Monitor each bird's performance closely, ensuring they are improving without signs of stress or fatigue.

Mental Conditioning for Races

Physical training is only part of the equation. Mental toughness and adaptability are just as important for racing success. Pigeons must learn to focus under pressure, adapt to unpredictable conditions, and navigate challenging routes.

- **Simulating Race Conditions**: To prepare pigeons for the intensity of races, replicate similar scenarios during training. Include longer distances, varied weather conditions, and unfamiliar release points.

- **Training in Adverse Weather**: While it's important not to endanger your birds, occasional training in light rain, moderate wind, or overcast skies can help them build resilience and confidence in less-than-ideal conditions.

- **Avoiding Overtraining**: Striking the right balance is crucial. Overtraining can lead to exhaustion and diminished performance. Monitor each bird's energy levels and adjust training schedules as needed.

- **Building Focus**: Minimize distractions during training sessions by choosing quiet release locations and maintaining a consistent routine. Pigeons thrive on predictability and structure.

Mental conditioning ensures that your pigeons are not only physically prepared but also mentally equipped to handle the demands of competitive racing.

Training a racing pigeon is a gradual process that combines physical conditioning, mental preparation, and strategic planning. By starting with the basics, progressing through systematic distance training, and simulating race conditions, you can mold your pigeons into formidable competitors.

CHAPTER SIX

MASTERING BREEDING FOR CHAMPIONS

The foundation of a successful pigeon racing loft lies in its breeding program. By carefully selecting breeding pairs, tracking genetic traits, and nurturing the next generation, you can develop a lineage of champions that embody both physical prowess and mental acuity. This chapter explores the art and science of breeding, guiding you through the essential steps to build a legacy of winning pigeons.

Selective Breeding Techniques

Selective breeding is the cornerstone of developing pigeons with the traits necessary for racing success. It involves pairing birds that exhibit superior genetics and complementary characteristics.

- **Identifying Desired Traits**: Look for pigeons with proven performance in races, excellent homing instincts, strong wings, and robust health. Behavioral traits, such as focus and adaptability, are equally important.

- **Balancing Genetics**: Pairing two strong birds does not guarantee superior offspring. Avoid overemphasizing a single trait, such as speed, at the expense of endurance or health. Instead, aim for balance in physical and mental attributes.

- **Line Breeding**: A common technique among pigeon racers, line breeding involves pairing birds that share a common ancestor to reinforce desirable traits. This should be done cautiously to avoid inbreeding-related health issues.

- **Outcrossing**: Occasionally introducing new bloodlines can prevent genetic stagnation and infuse fresh strengths into your loft. Select outcrosses with a proven history of performance.

Selective breeding requires patience and meticulous observation. It may take several generations to consistently produce pigeons with the desired combination of traits.

Tracking Pedigrees and Performance

Keeping detailed records of your pigeons' pedigrees and racing performance is vital for a successful breeding program. These records allow you to identify patterns and make informed decisions.

- **Pedigree Documentation**: Maintain comprehensive lineage records for every pigeon in your loft. Include information about parents, grandparents, and notable ancestors, along with their racing achievements.

- **Performance Metrics**: Track each bird's race results, including distances, times, and conditions. Consistent performance under varied circumstances is a hallmark of strong genetics.

- **Software Tools**: Modern technology offers tools for tracking and analyzing pedigrees and performance. Specialized pigeon management software can simplify the process and provide valuable insights.

- **Evaluating Results**: Breeding is an iterative process. Regularly review your outcomes and adjust pairings as needed to refine your bloodline.

These records are more than just data; they are a blueprint for future success, helping you identify and replicate the traits that lead to champions.

Caring for Eggs and Squabs

The health of the next generation begins even before the eggs are laid. Proper care during the breeding and rearing phases is critical to ensure strong, healthy offspring.

- **Breeding Environment**: Provide a clean, quiet, and well-ventilated loft for breeding pairs. Ensure they have ample space, nesting materials, and access to high-quality nutrition.

- **Egg Care**: Inspect eggs regularly to ensure they are fertile and undamaged. Use a candling lamp to check for developing embryos around five days after laying. Handle eggs gently to avoid breakage.

- **Incubation Support**: While pigeons naturally incubate their eggs, monitor the process to ensure consistency. Eggs should remain warm and protected from drafts.

- **Feeding Squabs**: Newly hatched squabs rely entirely on their parents for nutrition. Ensure the breeding pairs are well-fed with a diet rich in protein and calcium to produce nutrient-dense crop milk.

- **Monitoring Growth**: Observe squabs closely during the first few weeks of life. Healthy squabs should gain weight steadily, have smooth skin, and develop clean, vibrant feathers. Address any signs of illness or slow growth promptly.

By prioritizing the well-being of eggs and squabs, you set the stage for their development into strong, competitive pigeons.

Mastering breeding for champions is a blend of strategy, science, and care. By selecting superior pairs, tracking genetics and performance, and nurturing the next generation with diligence, you can establish a line of pigeons that excels on the racecourse. Breeding is both a responsibility and an opportunity to leave a lasting mark on the world of pigeon racing.

CHAPTER SEVEN

RACE DAY PREPARATION

The excitement of race day is the culmination of weeks, months, or even years of dedication and training. But as any experienced pigeon racer knows, the final preparation steps leading up to the race are just as crucial as the training that came before. How you manage your pigeons in the final hours before the race can be the difference between a champion and an also-ran. This chapter delves into the essential steps of pre-race conditioning, stress management, and how to factor in weather and route planning to maximize your pigeons' performance.

Pre-Race Conditioning

In the days leading up to a race, conditioning is all about fine-tuning the pigeons' physical and mental state to ensure they are in peak form when the starting gun goes off. It's the final push after all the hard work of training and breeding, and it demands careful attention.

- **Tapering the Training**: In the final week before the race, it's important to taper off the intensity of training. Pigeons should be well-rested and not fatigued. Avoid long flights or strenuous exercises in the days leading up to the race, as this can exhaust them and impact their performance.

- **Feeding Adjustments**: Pigeons need to be at their optimal weight for performance. In the days before the race, slightly reduce the amount of feed and focus on providing high-energy foods that will give them stamina without overloading their systems. A small increase in carbohydrates, like a little extra corn, can provide additional energy for the race.

- **Rest and Recovery**: Allow your pigeons ample time to rest in the days before the race. The night before the race, give them a good night's sleep in their loft. A well-rested bird will have more energy, agility, and focus during the race.

- **Mental Conditioning**: Mental sharpness is just as important as physical readiness. Keep the loft environment calm and quiet in the days leading up to the race. Pigeons are sensitive to stress and any disruptions can impact their focus.

By ensuring your pigeons are physically rested and mentally sharp, you give them the best chance to excel on race day.

Managing Stress and Rest

Racing pigeons are remarkably tough, but they are also highly sensitive to stress. Race day can be an intense experience for your pigeons, and how you manage their stress leading up to the release can have a significant impact on their performance.

- **Calm Environment**: Stress can be detrimental to performance, so it's essential to keep the environment as calm as possible before the race. Avoid loud noises, sudden changes in temperature, or any disruptions that might stress the pigeons out.

- **Pre-Race Handling**: Handle your pigeons as gently and calmly as possible before the race. In the final moments before release, pigeons should not feel rushed or panicked. Allow them time to settle and focus.

- **Hydration and Rest**: Ensure your pigeons are well-hydrated in the lead-up to the race. Dehydration can impair performance, especially during long-distance flights. Make sure they have access to fresh water up until the final moments before they are transported to the race site.

- **Travel Conditions**: If your pigeons are being transported to the race location, ensure that the journey is as stress-free as possible. A smooth, calm journey with adequate ventilation will help reduce anxiety. Make stops if necessary to allow the pigeons to rest during the journey.

By managing your pigeons' stress levels effectively, you will help them remain calm and focused, ready to face the race without being distracted by anxiety.

The Role of Weather and Route Planning

Weather conditions and route planning are two of the most unpredictable factors on race day, yet they have a significant impact on the outcome of the race. Understanding these environmental elements can give you a strategic advantage and help you predict how your pigeons will perform.

- **Weather Forecasting**: Weather plays a crucial role in pigeon racing. Wind, temperature, and humidity can all affect a pigeon's speed, endurance, and navigational accuracy. Strong headwinds, for instance, can slow pigeons down, while tailwinds can help them reach their lofts more quickly.

  - **Wind Conditions**: Headwinds can slow pigeons down, so it's important to factor this into your expectations for race times. On the other hand, tailwinds can provide a natural boost, allowing pigeons to race faster than expected.

- **Temperature and Humidity**: Extreme heat or cold can drain a pigeon's energy. In hot conditions, dehydration is a significant risk, while in cold weather, pigeons may struggle to maintain body temperature and stamina.

- **Route Planning**: Each race route presents unique challenges. Familiarizing yourself with the terrain, the winds, and any potential hazards along the route can help you better understand how your pigeons might perform. Consider how your pigeons will navigate over landmarks, bodies of water, or cityscapes, which might challenge their homing instincts.

  - **Understanding Geography**: Routes that involve crossing unfamiliar terrain or areas with significant weather challenges can add complexity to the race. A well-planned route that takes into account natural landmarks and wind patterns will help you predict how your pigeons will navigate.

  - **Timing Your Release**: Optimal release timing can be critical. Consider how the time of day, wind conditions, and temperature will affect the pigeons' ability to fly efficiently. Releasing pigeons during a period of calm weather conditions can maximize their chances for success.

By considering these weather and route factors, you can better assess the conditions your pigeons will face on race day and adjust your expectations accordingly.

Race day is a culmination of all the training, preparation, and care you've invested in your pigeons. The steps you take in the final hours before the race — from conditioning and stress management to understanding the weather and route — will determine how your pigeons perform. Successful race day preparation requires a combination of strategy, observation, and flexibility. By following the guidelines in this chapter, you will be ready to ensure that your pigeons are calm, focused, and physically prepared for the challenges ahead.

CHAPTER EIGHT

PIGEON RACING STRATEGIES

While pigeon racing is often about training, preparation, and conditioning, it's equally about strategy. The decisions you make leading up to, during, and after a race can dramatically impact your results. Understanding the competition, developing a winning strategy, and incorporating modern tools are essential elements in achieving success. In this chapter, we explore how to read the competition, develop your own race strategy, and use advanced technology to enhance your pigeon racing performance.

Reading the Competition

A significant aspect of pigeon racing that separates seasoned competitors from novices is the ability to read and understand your competition. Observing other racers' approaches can provide valuable insights that can help you fine-tune your own strategy.

- **Studying Training Techniques**: Successful pigeon racers often follow specific training regimens for their birds. By paying attention to how other racers train their pigeons, you can learn about different methods of conditioning and timing. Look for patterns in how they manage their pigeons before races—whether they prefer short training flights, how they adjust diets during peak season, or the types of lofts they use.

- **Race Day Rituals**: Every racer has their own pre-race routines, and many successful racers are deeply superstitious or highly systematic in their approach. Observing how they prepare their pigeons the night before, how they travel, and how they handle their birds in the final moments before release can give you insights into how they believe their birds perform best.

- **Understanding Other Racers' Weaknesses**: Analyzing your competition isn't just about learning their strengths, but also understanding their weaknesses. For example, some racers may overly rely on one aspect of pigeon performance—such as speed—while neglecting others like endurance or mental resilience. By knowing where they may fall short, you can better prepare your pigeons to take advantage of these gaps.

- **Collaborating with Other Racers**: While pigeon racing is a competitive sport, many experienced racers collaborate and share knowledge. Joining a local club or community can help you gain insight into strategies that others have found successful. It also gives you a chance to learn from their mistakes and avoid pitfalls that could cost you the race.

Being able to analyze your competition and adjust your strategy accordingly is a critical skill that can give you an edge on race day.

Developing a Winning Strategy

In pigeon racing, strategy isn't just about speed; it's about balance. The key to success lies in finding the right combination of speed, endurance, and risk management. Here's how to develop a strategy that will put your pigeons in the best position for success.

- **Balancing Speed and Endurance**: Pigeons are typically faster than most other birds, but their stamina is what gets them to the finish line first.

While speed is important for a competitive edge, it's endurance that ultimately wins races, especially in longer competitions. Developing a strategy means finding a balance between these two elements. In shorter races, you may focus more on speed, while in longer races, endurance becomes paramount.

- **Taking Calculated Risks**: Every race presents an opportunity for strategic decisions. Whether it's the timing of a release or how aggressively you push your pigeons to train, sometimes success comes down to taking calculated risks. However, the most successful racers know when to hold back and when to go for broke. Overtraining, too early releases, or poor weather decisions can all cost you, so ensure your strategy is one that factors in both short-term and long-term consequences.

- **Knowing When to Push the Birds**: Understanding when to push your pigeons to their limit is key. Pushing them too hard in training or making aggressive race decisions without assessing their physical condition can harm your long-term performance. A great strategy ensures your pigeons are not pushed beyond their limits until they are ready.

- **Managing the Recovery Period**: After each race, rest and recovery are essential components of a winning strategy. Allowing pigeons adequate time to rest, rehydrate, and refuel helps them perform at their best in the next competition. Successful racers often emphasize recovery, ensuring that their pigeons stay in optimal health and mental condition for future races.

By developing a well-rounded strategy that balances risk, speed, endurance, and recovery, you give your pigeons the best opportunity to come out on top.

Using Modern Tools: Electronic Timing Systems

Technology has revolutionized the world of pigeon racing. While traditional timing methods are still in use, modern tools like electronic timing systems are now a staple for serious racers, offering enhanced accuracy and efficiency. Here's how these systems work and why they are indispensable for any competitive racer.

- **Electronic Rings and Timing Chips**: Electronic rings are used to track pigeons as they pass through designated checkpoints. These rings are equipped with microchips that transmit data to timing systems. As the pigeon arrives at the loft, the system records the time of arrival and can instantly compare it to the timing of competitors. This level of precision is invaluable for reducing the margin of error.

- **Real-Time Data and Tracking**: Advanced timing systems often integrate with GPS to track pigeons during their race. These systems can record the bird's flight path, speed, and distance, allowing racers to monitor their pigeons' performance in real time. This is especially useful for assessing how pigeons respond to weather conditions, terrain, and other environmental factors.

- **Accurate Results and Fairness**: Traditional timing systems required the manual recording of times, which could be prone to errors or inaccuracies. With electronic timing, results are instant and highly accurate, reducing the potential for disputes. Every pigeon's performance can be tracked with precision, ensuring fairness for all participants.

- **Training Feedback**: Electronic timing systems aren't just for race day; they can also provide valuable feedback for training. By measuring your pigeons' times over various training distances, you can identify patterns and assess the impact of different training strategies. This helps you fine-tune your approach and optimize your pigeons' performance for future races.

Using modern tools like electronic timing systems can enhance every aspect of your pigeon racing strategy, giving you an edge over competitors who may rely solely on traditional methods. These tools offer more accuracy, faster results, and a level of analysis that can improve both training and race-day performance.

In pigeon racing, the difference between winning and losing often comes down to strategy. Understanding your competition, developing a balanced race plan, and leveraging modern technology can dramatically improve your chances of success. By analyzing your competitors, weighing the risks, and incorporating electronic tools for precision timing, you place yourself in the best position to race for the win.

CHAPTER NINE

HEALTH AND WELLNESS FOR RACING PIGEONS

The health and well-being of your racing pigeons are paramount to their performance. Ensuring that they are in peak condition year-round requires not only proper care and training but also vigilance in identifying and managing any health issues. In this chapter, we will focus on preventative care, recognizing and treating common ailments, and implementing effective recovery strategies to keep your pigeons in top form.

Preventative Care Essentials

Preventative care is the foundation of a healthy pigeon, ensuring that birds stay fit, strong, and able to race effectively. Regular practices can prevent many common issues before they even begin, so consistency is key.

- **Daily Health Checks**: Start each day by inspecting your pigeons. Check for signs of abnormal behavior, poor feather condition, changes in appetite, or signs of injury. Early detection of problems can help prevent them from escalating into more severe health issues.

- **Maintaining a Clean Loft**: A clean, dry, and well-ventilated loft is crucial for preventing respiratory infections and other diseases. Ensure that droppings are removed daily and that bedding is regularly replaced. Proper sanitation can also help reduce the risk of parasites and pests that can affect your pigeons' health.

- **Proper Nutrition**: A balanced diet is one of the most important elements in keeping your pigeons healthy. Offer a variety of grains, vitamins, minerals, and fresh water to meet their nutritional needs. Tailor their diet based on their training schedule and performance needs.

- **Vaccination and Disease Prevention**: Regular vaccinations are essential to protect your pigeons from diseases like avian influenza, Newcastle disease, and other common pigeon illnesses. Work with your veterinarian to establish a vaccination schedule and to discuss any potential health risks in your area.

- **Foot and Beak Care**: Regular checks of the feet and beaks are vital. Look for signs of infection or abnormalities such as scabs, swelling, or cracks. Pigeons that race often can develop issues such as footpad sores or damaged beaks, so these should be addressed promptly.

By establishing a solid routine of preventative care, you can ensure that your pigeons are healthy, active, and ready for training or competition.

Recognizing Common Ailments

Even with the best preventative care, racing pigeons may still face health challenges. Understanding the symptoms of common ailments is essential for quick identification and treatment.

- **Respiratory Infections**: One of the most common health issues in pigeons, respiratory infections can be caused by bacterial, viral, or fungal pathogens. Signs include wheezing, coughing, nasal discharge, or labored breathing. If you notice any of these symptoms, isolate the affected bird immediately to prevent the infection from spreading to other pigeons. A veterinarian will likely prescribe antibiotics or antifungal treatments.

- **Parasites and Mites**: Pigeons are susceptible to internal and external parasites, such as worms, lice, and mites. External parasites often cause itching, feather loss, and skin irritation. Internal parasites may lead to weight loss, diarrhea, or lethargy. Regular deworming and applying mite treatment to their environment can help manage these issues.

- **Fatigue and Overtraining**: Sometimes pigeons show signs of fatigue from overtraining or being pushed too hard before a race. Symptoms include lethargy, reduced appetite, and difficulty flying. To prevent overtraining, establish a balanced schedule that incorporates adequate rest between training sessions. If fatigue becomes an issue, allow extra time for recovery and adjust training intensity.

- **Injuries**: Racing pigeons are prone to injury, especially when training in harsh conditions or during races. Injuries can occur during flight or as a result of collisions. Common injuries include broken wings, fractured toes, and muscle strains. If you suspect an injury, assess the bird's condition and consult a veterinarian if needed. Depending on the injury, treatment could range from rest to more involved procedures such as bandaging or splinting.

- **Digestive Problems**: Pigeons can experience digestive issues due to poor diet or stress. Symptoms might include diarrhea, vomiting, or a change in droppings. A varied and balanced diet can help prevent digestive issues, but if symptoms persist, consult a veterinarian for further guidance.

Recognizing these common ailments early can help you address the issues promptly, preventing them from affecting your pigeons' performance.

Recovery and Rehabilitation

Post-race recovery is just as important as training. After a challenging race, your pigeons will need time to recuperate. Recovery and rehabilitation ensure that your birds return to peak condition quickly, reducing the risk of burnout or injury.

- **Rest and Hydration**: After a race, pigeons should be given ample time to rest. Provide a quiet, comfortable space where they can relax and recover. Ensure they have access to fresh water, and consider adding electrolytes to their water to help with hydration and recovery. Dehydration can severely impact a bird's ability to recover, so it's important to monitor water intake during this time.

- **Nutrition for Recovery**: During recovery, provide your pigeons with high-quality food to rebuild muscle tissue and replenish energy stores. Foods high in proteins, such as peas, lentils, and maize, help with tissue repair, while carbohydrates will restore lost energy. For birds that have raced for long distances, providing additional fats and amino acids can also be beneficial.

- **Gentle Exercise**: While rest is vital, gentle exercise is also important to prevent stiffness and promote muscle recovery. Once your pigeons have had adequate rest, allow them short, light flights to gradually regain their strength. This helps improve circulation and reduces muscle fatigue.

- **Massage and Physical Therapy**: Just as athletes undergo physiotherapy, pigeons can benefit from gentle massages and stretches to ease muscle tension and reduce soreness. Be gentle when handling your pigeons, as excessive pressure can lead to injury. Massage can be particularly effective after long races to reduce strain on their muscles.

- **Monitoring Health Post-Race**: Even after the race, keep a close eye on your pigeons. If you notice signs of continued fatigue, stress, or any new health issues, consult a veterinarian. Prolonged recovery times or failure to regain full strength can indicate underlying health issues that need attention.

A comprehensive recovery strategy ensures that your pigeons return to training in peak condition, ready for the next race. Incorporating rest, proper nutrition, hydration, and gradual rehabilitation helps your pigeons bounce back stronger and more resilient than before.

Maintaining the health and wellness of your racing pigeons is a year-round responsibility that involves regular preventative care, being proactive in recognizing and treating ailments, and offering effective recovery methods. By staying vigilant, you can prevent many common health issues from affecting your pigeons' performance. Whether it's daily maintenance, managing injuries, or aiding recovery after a race, ensuring the health of your pigeons is essential to their long-term success

CHAPTER TEN

COMPETING AND THRIVING IN RACING CLUBS

As a pigeon racer, being part of a racing club can significantly enhance your experience and success. These clubs offer a supportive community, valuable resources, and a structured environment where you can compete, learn, and grow. In this chapter, we will explore the benefits of joining a racing club, understanding race regulations, and how to network and build relationships within the pigeon racing community.

Joining a Racing Club

Being a member of a racing club provides numerous advantages for both beginners and experienced racers. Clubs bring together like-minded individuals who share the same passion for pigeon racing. By joining a racing club, you open the door to a wealth of knowledge, support, and opportunities to improve your skills.

- **Access to Resources**: Racing clubs often offer resources that can be invaluable in your pigeon racing journey. These can include training sessions, expert advice, and sometimes even discounts on pigeon-related products and services. Many clubs also offer access to experienced racers who can guide you in the right direction when it comes to breeding, training, and race preparation.

- **Opportunities to Compete**: Racing clubs organize local and regional competitions, which give you the chance to test your pigeons against others in a structured and fair environment. These competitions are not only exciting but also provide a benchmark for your progress. As a club member, you'll be able to participate in these events and learn from your results to improve your strategy for future races.

- **Mentorship and Learning**: For new racers, joining a club provides an invaluable opportunity to learn from experienced individuals. Mentorship is a key aspect of club membership. Veteran racers often take the time to share their knowledge, offering tips on training, nutrition, and other aspects of pigeon racing. Their experience can help you avoid common pitfalls and accelerate your progress.

When considering which racing club to join, research local clubs, their reputations, and the services they offer. Many clubs also have an online presence, making it easy to communicate and find like-minded individuals even if you're far from the club's physical location.

Navigating Race Regulations

Understanding and adhering to race regulations is crucial for ensuring fair competition and the success of your pigeons. Every racing event has specific rules and guidelines that must be followed, and it's essential to familiarize yourself with them to avoid penalties or disqualification.

- **General Race Rules**: Racing pigeon regulations may vary depending on the event and location, but some general rules are consistent across the sport. These often include guidelines on pigeon identification (such as banding), race distances, and the time frame for pigeons to return. Make sure your pigeons are properly banded with legal identification tags, as failure to do so could result in disqualification.

- **Fair Play and Ethics**: Each race is designed to be a fair competition, and all racers must adhere to the same rules. For example, tampering with the pigeons or engaging in unethical practices can result in severe consequences. Clubs often have ethical codes that members are expected to follow to maintain the integrity of the sport.

- **Specific Race Regulations**: Some races may have additional specific rules related to race routes, weather conditions, or the use of technology, such as GPS tracking. It is important to carefully read the regulations for each event to ensure you understand what is expected and how to prepare your pigeons accordingly.

- **Legal Considerations**: In some areas, there may be legal regulations governing pigeon racing. These might include restrictions on the types of pigeons that can be raced, race frequencies, or even zoning laws related to lofts and pigeon housing. It's essential to stay informed about any local laws that may impact your participation in races.

Staying well-informed about race regulations and ensuring compliance is a key aspect of being a successful and respected member of the racing community.

Building Community and Networking

One of the most rewarding aspects of joining a racing club is the sense of community it offers. The pigeon racing world is vast and diverse, and building relationships within this community can help you grow as a racer and enrich your experience.

- **Learning from Others**: Racing clubs are filled with individuals who have a wealth of knowledge, ranging from beginners to seasoned experts. Take advantage of this by engaging with your fellow club members. Ask questions, share your experiences, and learn from the successes and challenges of others. This exchange of ideas and knowledge will not only help you become a better racer but also foster a supportive environment where everyone benefits.

- **Attending Events and Socials**: Many racing clubs organize events beyond just races, including social gatherings, workshops, and training seminars. These events provide great opportunities to meet other racers, hear from experts, and participate in discussions that can enhance your understanding of the sport. By attending these events, you position yourself to make valuable connections with other racers and industry experts.

- **Collaborating with Fellow Racers**: Networking within the racing community can lead to collaborations that may significantly improve your racing success. For instance, you might exchange tips on breeding strategies, share insights on race routes, or even train together to better prepare your pigeons. Working with others who have similar goals can accelerate your growth and open up new opportunities.

- **International Networking**: Pigeon racing is a global sport, and many racers maintain strong international networks. Being part of a club can connect you to racers from different parts of the world, allowing you to exchange strategies, learn about international competitions, and discuss the global state of the sport. This can broaden your horizons and help you adapt to new challenges and trends in pigeon racing.

Building relationships and actively participating in the pigeon racing community not only enhances your skills but also enriches your experience. The friendships and networks you develop through a racing club can become long-lasting and impactful in your racing career.

Joining a racing club is one of the best decisions you can make to further your career as a pigeon racer. It provides access to a wealth of resources, mentorship, and opportunities to compete. Understanding race regulations ensures that you participate in a fair and ethical manner, while building community ties within the racing world allows you to learn, grow, and thrive. As you continue to develop your skills, being an active member of a racing club will keep you engaged, motivated, and connected to a supportive network of fellow racers.

CHAPTER ELEVEN

RECORD-KEEPING AND PERFORMANCE ANALYSIS

In pigeon racing, success is as much about data as it is about training and care. Accurate record-keeping and performance analysis are essential tools for identifying strengths, addressing weaknesses, and improving results over time. In this chapter, we will explore how to track individual pigeon stats, analyze results for improvement, and utilize digital tools to streamline the management of your racing records.

Tracking Individual Pigeon Stats

Every pigeon in your loft is unique, with its own set of strengths, weaknesses, and tendencies. By keeping detailed records of each bird's performance, health, and breeding history, you can make informed decisions that enhance your overall racing program.

- **Flight Performance**: Record distances flown, times, and rankings in each race. Monitoring these metrics over time helps you identify high-performing pigeons and those that may need additional training or rest. Keep notes on flight conditions, as weather and wind can significantly affect performance.

- **Health and Wellness Logs**: Documenting health checks, treatments, and vaccinations ensures that you maintain a healthy loft. Regular records of weight, feather condition, and appetite can signal early signs of illness or stress.

- **Breeding History**: Track which pairs produce the most successful offspring. Include details about hatch dates, parentage, and squab development milestones. This information is crucial for making informed decisions about future breeding plans.

- **Behavioral Observations**: Note any peculiar habits or behaviors, such as a pigeon's reaction to stress or its ability to adapt to new training routines. Behavioral insights can provide clues to a bird's racing potential and psychological resilience.

Using a dedicated notebook, spreadsheet, or digital platform, create a structured format for recording these details. Consistency is key, as small patterns or trends might only become evident after months or years of data collection.

Analyzing Results for Improvement

Once you've collected data, the next step is to analyze it systematically. This process will help you understand what's working, where improvements can be made, and how to adjust your strategies for better outcomes.

- **Identifying High Performers**: Look for patterns in your data to identify pigeons that consistently excel under specific conditions, such as long distances, headwinds, or certain race routes. These insights can inform training and breeding decisions.

- **Pinpointing Weaknesses**: By analyzing poor performances, you can uncover issues such as insufficient conditioning, suboptimal nutrition, or health problems. This enables you to take targeted corrective action.

- **Comparing Training Methods**: Evaluate the effectiveness of different training routines by comparing results over time. For example, you might test whether short, frequent training flights yield better results than longer, less frequent ones.

- **Adapting to External Factors**: Use race data to assess how external conditions—such as weather, altitude, or release times—impact your pigeons. Adjust your strategies accordingly to give your birds the best possible chance of success.

The insights gained from analyzing your records not only improve individual performances but also elevate your overall loft management practices.

Using Apps and Software for Record Management

In today's digital age, technology has revolutionized pigeon racing. A growing number of apps and software programs are specifically designed to help racers manage records and analyze performance data efficiently.

- **Key Features of Digital Tools**: Most apps allow you to track individual pigeon stats, log race results, and generate performance reports. Some even integrate with electronic timing systems, automatically recording race times and rankings.

- **Data Organization**: Digital platforms make it easier to store and organize large volumes of data. With just a few clicks, you can access a pigeon's complete history, compare results, or generate summaries for breeding or training purposes.

- **Advanced Analytics**: Many tools include built-in analytics features, such as performance graphs, predictive modeling, and trend analysis. These capabilities help you make data-driven decisions quickly and accurately.

- **Popular Options**: Explore tools such as PigeonPlanner, WinRace, or specialized apps provided by racing clubs. These platforms are user-friendly and cater to the unique needs of pigeon racers.

While digital tools offer many advantages, it's important to back up your data regularly to avoid losing valuable records. Combining digital tools with physical backups, such as printed reports, ensures that your information remains secure.

Record-keeping and performance analysis are the cornerstones of successful pigeon racing. By meticulously tracking individual stats, analyzing results, and leveraging modern digital tools, you gain a deeper understanding of your pigeons' abilities and how to enhance their performance. This chapter has outlined practical methods for managing your records and using them to achieve consistent improvement. In the next chapter, we will delve into the ethical considerations and responsibilities that come with pigeon racing, ensuring the sport remains fair, humane, and rewarding for everyone involved.

CHAPTER TWELVE

ETHICS AND RESPONSIBILITIES IN PIGEON RACING

Pigeon racing is a sport steeped in tradition and respect, not only for the competition but for the birds that make it possible. As racers, breeders, and caretakers, it is our duty to ensure that the welfare of our pigeons takes precedence over personal ambition. This chapter focuses on the ethical responsibilities of pigeon racing, emphasizing humane treatment, balanced training practices, and the importance of sportsmanship.

Promoting Humane Treatment

The cornerstone of ethical pigeon racing lies in treating pigeons with care, respect, and compassion. These birds are more than competitors—they are living beings entrusted to our stewardship.

- **Proper Living Conditions**: Ensure that your loft is spacious, clean, and well-ventilated. Overcrowding can lead to stress, disease, and diminished performance. A comfortable living environment not only supports health but also fosters trust between pigeons and their caregivers.

- **Health and Nutrition**: Prioritize your birds' health by providing a balanced diet, clean water, and regular medical check-ups. Avoid using performance-enhancing substances that could compromise their well-being.

- **Gentle Handling Practices**: Minimize stress during training, handling, and transport. Gentle interactions build trust, which can improve performance and create a deeper bond between you and your pigeons.

By promoting humane treatment, you not only honor your pigeons but also uphold the integrity of the sport.

Avoiding Overtraining and Over racing

Ambition is a natural part of competition, but pushing pigeons too hard can lead to burnout, injuries, and long-term health issues. Finding the right balance between training and rest is essential for their well-being.

- **Signs of Overtraining**: Monitor your pigeons for signs of exhaustion, such as reluctance to fly, decreased appetite, or sluggish behavior. Recognizing these signals early can prevent more serious issues.

- **Adequate Rest Periods**: Incorporate rest days into your training schedule and avoid scheduling back-to-back races. Rest allows pigeons to recover both physically and mentally, ensuring sustained performance over time.

- **Seasonal Planning**: Limit the number of races each pigeon participates in during a season. Over racing can lead to cumulative fatigue and compromise their long-term health and racing potential.

Striking a balance between ambition and care not only safeguards your pigeons but also ensures their peak performance over multiple seasons.

The Importance of Sportsmanship

Pigeon racing is a community-driven sport that thrives on mutual respect, fairness, and camaraderie. Upholding the principles of good sportsmanship elevates the experience for everyone involved.

- **Fair Play**: Follow all competition rules and regulations, from proper timing protocols to ethical training practices. Cheating undermines the spirit of the sport and diminishes the value of true accomplishments.

- **Respect for Fellow Racers**: Celebrate the successes of others and share in the collective knowledge of the community. Supporting your peers fosters an environment of collaboration and mutual growth.

- **Setting a Positive Example**: As an experienced racer, you have the opportunity to mentor newcomers and promote ethical practices. By leading with integrity, you contribute to the long-term sustainability of the sport.

Good sportsmanship extends beyond the racecourse. It is reflected in how you treat your pigeons, engage with fellow racers, and represent the sport to the wider world.

Ethics and responsibilities are at the heart of pigeon racing. By ensuring humane treatment, avoiding overtraining, and embracing sportsmanship, you honor the pigeons that make the sport possible and contribute to a thriving, respectful community. These principles not only protect the welfare of the birds but also uphold the values that have defined pigeon racing for generations.

In the next chapter, we will explore how to share your passion for the sport with others and contribute to the growth of pigeon racing in the modern era.

CHAPTER THIRTEEN

ADVANCED TECHNIQUES FOR EXPERIENCED RACERS

For seasoned pigeon racers, the challenge lies in continually improving and mastering the complexities of the sport. As your experience grows, so too should your strategies, allowing you to push the boundaries of what your pigeons can achieve. This chapter dives into advanced techniques, covering long-distance racing tactics, conditioning for extreme weather, and advanced breeding methods to develop elite traits.

Long-Distance Racing Tactics

Races spanning hundreds of miles test not only the endurance of your pigeons but also your skills as a trainer and strategist. Preparing for such events requires meticulous planning and a focus on stamina.

- **Gradual Distance Increases**: Build your pigeons' endurance by systematically extending their training distances. Start with short flights, gradually moving to longer routes over several months.

- **Nutritional Preparation**: Tailor your feeding program to support sustained energy release. Include slow-digesting grains like maize and barley in pre-race meals, paired with high-protein recovery diets post-flight.

- **Mental Toughness**: Long-distance races can be mentally taxing for pigeons. Simulate challenging conditions during training, such as varied landscapes or isolated release points, to build their confidence and focus.

- **Route Familiarity**: If possible, familiarize your pigeons with key segments of the race route during training. Knowing the terrain can improve their efficiency and speed.

By combining physical and mental preparation, you can equip your pigeons to excel in the demanding arena of long-distance racing.

Conditioning for Extreme Weather

Weather conditions can make or break a race. Whether it's soaring temperatures, heavy rain, or strong winds, your pigeons need to be prepared to face the elements and thrive.

- **Training in Diverse Conditions**: Gradually introduce your pigeons to varied weather during training. Expose them to early morning flights with heavy dew, afternoon heat, and breezy evenings to build adaptability.

- **Hydration Strategies**: In hot climates, hydration is critical. Provide electrolyte solutions in water to prevent dehydration and maintain energy levels.

- **Cold Weather Considerations**: For colder regions, focus on diets rich in fats to provide extra energy. Ensure your loft is insulated and free from drafts to help pigeons recover post-race.

- **Weather Forecasting Skills**: Learn to interpret weather forecasts and their potential impact on race conditions. Adjust your training and racing strategies accordingly to minimize risks.

Adapting your training and care practices to account for weather variability ensures your pigeons remain competitive, no matter the forecast.

Advanced Breeding for Elite Traits

Experienced racers often turn to advanced breeding techniques to develop pigeons with exceptional capabilities. While genetics cannot replace training, the right pairings can significantly enhance performance potential.

- **Pairing for Specific Traits**: Identify pigeons with complementary strengths, such as stamina, speed, or navigational accuracy. Breeding these traits can create a lineage of well-rounded racers.

- **Pedigree Analysis**: Study the performance history of your pigeons' ancestors. Use data to make informed decisions about pairings, focusing on birds with consistent race success.

- **Hybrid Vigor**: Occasionally introduce fresh genetic lines to your loft. Crossbreeding unrelated pigeons can produce offspring with enhanced vigor and resilience.

- **Responsible Breeding**: Avoid overbreeding or prioritizing aesthetics over function. The health and welfare of your pigeons should always be the top priority.

Advanced breeding requires patience, record-keeping, and a deep understanding of pigeon genetics. When done responsibly, it can lead to remarkable results over time.

Mastering advanced techniques is a continuous journey that rewards dedication and innovation. Long-distance racing tactics, weather conditioning, and elite breeding strategies provide experienced racers with the tools to excel and push the limits of the sport. By combining these methods with your existing expertise, you can elevate your pigeons—and yourself—to new heights in competitive racing.

In the following chapter, we'll discuss how to share your expertise, mentor new racers, and leave a lasting legacy in the world of pigeon racing.

CHAPTER FOURTEEN

RESOURCES FOR ENTHUSIASTS

Pigeon racing is a dynamic and ever-evolving sport that thrives on community, shared knowledge, and a passion for continuous improvement. Whether you're a beginner eager to learn or a seasoned racer looking to expand your network, tapping into the right resources can greatly enhance your experience. This chapter provides a guide to pigeon racing clubs, recommended reading, online communities, and connecting with experts in the field.

Pigeon Racing Clubs and Associations

Joining a pigeon racing club or association is one of the most rewarding steps you can take as an enthusiast. These organizations provide access to competitions, resources, and like-minded individuals who share your passion.

- **Local Clubs**: Most regions have pigeon racing clubs that host events and offer support to members. These clubs are ideal for learning the ropes, meeting fellow racers, and participating in local races.

- **National and International Federations**: Organizations like the National Pigeon Association (NPA) and Federation Colombophile Internationale (FCI) bring together racers from across the globe. Membership often includes access to competitions, newsletters, and educational resources.

- **Youth Programs**: Some clubs offer programs specifically for younger enthusiasts, ensuring the sport continues to thrive across generations.

To find a club or association near you, search online directories or inquire within your local pigeon racing community. Becoming a member opens doors to valuable opportunities and connections.

Recommended Reading and Online Communities

The world of pigeon racing is rich with literature and digital platforms that cater to enthusiasts of all levels. These resources allow you to expand your knowledge and stay updated on the latest trends and techniques.

- **Books and Guides**: Many seasoned racers and experts have published books covering everything from training methods to advanced genetics. Popular titles include classics on pigeon care and contemporary works on modern racing techniques.

- **Blogs and Websites**: Websites dedicated to pigeon racing often feature articles, tutorials, and interviews with experts. Look for blogs maintained by experienced racers, as they often share unique insights.

- **Online Forums and Social Media Groups**: Platforms like Facebook, Reddit, and specialized pigeon racing forums offer spaces for enthusiasts to connect, share tips, and ask questions. These communities are invaluable for troubleshooting and learning from others' experiences.

Consistently engaging with these resources ensures that you stay informed and inspired throughout your pigeon racing journey.

Connecting with Experts

No resource is as valuable as the guidance of a seasoned expert. Mentorship provides hands-on insights that no book or online article can fully replicate.

- **Finding Mentors**: Experienced breeders, trainers, and racers often welcome the opportunity to share their knowledge. Attend club meetings, races, and pigeon exhibitions to meet potential mentors.

- **Learning Through Apprenticeship**: Offering to assist an expert with their loft and training routines is a great way to gain firsthand experience.

- **Workshops and Seminars**: Many clubs and federations host workshops where experts discuss advanced techniques and emerging trends in pigeon racing.

- **Virtual Consultations**: With advancements in technology, many experts are now accessible via online platforms. Virtual consultations allow you to seek advice regardless of your location.

Building a relationship with an expert accelerates your learning curve and gives you access to strategies and techniques that are honed over years of experience.

The beauty of pigeon racing lies in its strong sense of community and the wealth of resources available to those willing to seek them out. By joining clubs, diving into recommended readings, participating in online communities, and connecting with experts, you'll not only enhance your skills but also deepen your appreciation for the sport.

As you continue your journey, remember that learning never stops. Embrace every opportunity to grow, contribute, and share your passion with others. In the final chapter, we'll explore how to leave a lasting legacy in pigeon racing and inspire future generations of enthusiasts.

The Joy of Pigeon Racing

Pigeon racing is much more than a competitive sport; it is a deeply fulfilling pursuit that nurtures the bond between humans and their feathered athletes. The joy lies not just in the thrill of victory but in the small, everyday moments— watching pigeons gracefully return to their lofts, marveling at their endurance, and sharing stories with fellow fanciers.

This unique connection develops through hours of care, training, and trust-building. Fanciers often describe their pigeons as part of the family, each bird with its personality and quirks. Racing pigeons is an exercise in patience, dedication, and respect for these extraordinary creatures. The relationship is reciprocal; as we invest in their well-being, they reward us with loyalty, awe-inspiring performances, and unforgettable memories.

Beyond the races, pigeon fanciers find joy in the camaraderie of the community. Clubs, competitions, and shared experiences unite enthusiasts across generations, cultures, and continents. It's a hobby that turns strangers into lifelong friends, all bound by a shared love for these remarkable birds.

Lifelong Learning and Growth

Pigeon racing is a journey of constant discovery. No matter how much experience a fancier accumulates, there is always something new to learn—be it a breakthrough in nutrition, an innovative training method, or a fresh perspective from a fellow racer.

This culture of lifelong learning keeps the sport vibrant and rewarding. Fanciers are naturally curious and driven to improve, studying their birds' behavior, fine-tuning their strategies, and experimenting with new techniques. Even setbacks, such as losing a race or facing challenges in breeding, serve as valuable lessons that pave the way for growth.

The pursuit of excellence in pigeon racing extends beyond the loft. It teaches discipline, perseverance, and an appreciation for the intricate balance between nature and nurture. These lessons enrich not just the sport but also the lives of those who participate in it.

Inspiring the Next Generation

Every great tradition thrives when passed down to future generations, and pigeon racing is no exception. Encouraging young people to take an interest in the sport is vital for its continued growth and vitality.

Introducing children and teenagers to pigeon racing is an opportunity to teach them about responsibility, patience, and the joy of caring for animals. It's also a chance to foster curiosity about biology, geography, and even technology as they learn about breeding, navigation, and timing systems.

Mentorship plays a key role in inspiring newcomers. Sharing your knowledge, offering guidance, and involving younger family members or local youth groups in the care and training of pigeons can spark a lifelong passion. Many clubs have programs designed to engage young enthusiasts, offering mentorships and starter kits to make it easier for them to enter the sport.

Social media and modern communication tools also provide platforms to reach and inspire a broader audience. By sharing stories, achievements, and insights, you can showcase the beauty and excitement of pigeon racing to people who might not otherwise be exposed to it.

Pigeon racing is more than a pastime; it is a celebration of life's simple yet profound joys. From the bond between fanciers and their birds to the personal growth it inspires and the legacy it fosters for future generations, the sport has a timeless appeal that transcends competition.

By cherishing these aspects and sharing them with others, we ensure that pigeon racing remains not only relevant but also deeply cherished for years to come. Whether you are a seasoned fancier or a newcomer to the sport, you are part of a tradition that is as rewarding as it is enduring. Embrace the journey, share the joy, and continue to inspire.

CHAPTER FIFTEEN

THE ECONOMICS OF PIGEON RACING

Pigeon racing, like any passion, requires a thoughtful approach to managing its financial aspects. Understanding the costs, exploring financial opportunities, and learning how to budget effectively are essential for anyone aiming to thrive in this rewarding yet resource-intensive sport.

Costs of Pigeon Racing

Pigeon racing entails a variety of expenses, ranging from initial setup to ongoing care and competition costs. For newcomers, it's crucial to grasp the financial commitment involved:

1. **Loft   Setup**:
   Building a loft is often the most significant upfront expense. The cost depends on factors such as size, materials, and features like ventilation and security. While custom-built lofts can be pricey, many fanciers opt for DIY solutions to save money.

2. **Feed   and   Nutrition**:
   Providing high-quality feed is non-negotiable for maintaining your pigeons' health and performance. Seasonal variations, such as energy-rich diets during racing seasons, may slightly increase costs. Supplements like vitamins and electrolytes also add to this category.

3. **Healthcare**:
   Regular health checks, vaccinations, and treatments for common ailments are necessary investments. Prevention is often more cost-effective than dealing with illnesses or injuries after the fact.

4. **Competition** **Fees**:
    Entering races, joining clubs, and participating in events come with fees. While these costs can add up, they are often justified by the experience, networking, and potential rewards they bring.

5. **Miscellaneous** **Costs**:
    Training baskets, electronic timing systems, and transportation to and from race sites are additional expenses to consider.

Financial Opportunities in Racing

While pigeon racing involves costs, it also offers opportunities for financial gain. Experienced fanciers often find ways to offset expenses or even generate income through the following avenues:

1. **Prize** **Money**:
    Winning races can bring significant financial rewards. Prestigious competitions often have substantial cash prizes, making them lucrative for skilled racers.

2. **Breeding** **and** **Selling**:
    Breeding champion pigeons can be highly profitable. Offspring from proven racers often fetch high prices, particularly if their lineage is well-documented. This is a common way for fanciers to monetize their expertise and successful bloodlines.

3. **Consulting** **and** **Mentorship**:
    Seasoned fanciers may offer training, breeding, or loft management advice to newcomers for a fee. This not only helps others but also creates a supplementary income stream.

4. **Sponsorships and Partnerships**:
   As the sport grows in popularity, some fanciers secure sponsorships from businesses or collaborate with organizations to promote events and products.

Budgeting Tips for New Racers

For those new to pigeon racing, managing costs wisely is critical. Here are some practical tips to help you get started without overspending:

1. **Start Small**:
   Begin with a modest loft and a small number of pigeons. Focus on building your skills and experience before scaling up.

2. **DIY Where Possible**:
   From constructing your loft to making training baskets, many aspects of pigeon racing can be done yourself to save money.

3. **Plan Ahead**:
   Anticipate seasonal expenses like vaccines, racing fees, and feed adjustments. Creating a yearly budget can help you avoid surprises.

4. **Buy Smart**:
   Invest in quality over quantity when selecting pigeons, feed, and equipment. Opting for cheaper alternatives often leads to higher costs in the long run.

5. **Leverage Clubs and Communities**:
   Joining a pigeon racing club not only provides valuable advice but also offers access to shared resources like bulk feed purchases and discounted equipment.

Understanding the economics of pigeon racing ensures that the sport remains sustainable and enjoyable. By balancing costs, exploring financial opportunities, and adopting smart budgeting strategies, you can focus on what truly matters—nurturing your pigeons and excelling in the sport.

Whether you're an aspiring enthusiast or a seasoned racer, a solid financial foundation will enable you to pursue pigeon racing with confidence and passion for years to come.

CHAPTER SIXTEEN

LEGAL AND ETHICAL CONSIDERATIONS

Pigeon racing is not just a sport; it is a tradition steeped in respect for both the birds and the fanciers who raise them. As the sport continues to evolve, legal and ethical considerations play an increasingly important role in ensuring its integrity, sustainability, and humane practices. Understanding these aspects is essential for all participants, from newcomers to seasoned experts.

Regulations Governing Pigeon Racing

Racing pigeons involves adherence to a framework of local and international laws designed to protect the welfare of birds and maintain fair competition. Some key areas of regulation include:

1. **Animal Welfare Laws**: Many countries have specific guidelines on the care, housing, and treatment of racing pigeons. Ensuring that your loft meets these standards is not only a legal requirement but also an ethical obligation.

2. **Race Entry Requirements**: Each club or organization may have its own rules regarding the eligibility of pigeons, registration processes, and vaccination protocols. Familiarizing yourself with these standards helps avoid disqualification or disputes.

3. **Transportation and Release Protocols**: Laws governing the transportation of animals, particularly across borders, often apply to racing pigeons. Compliance with quarantine regulations

and health certifications is essential for international competitors.

4. **Environmental Regulations**: Pigeon racing organizers must often consider environmental impacts, such as the release of large flocks in sensitive areas. Understanding these regulations helps preserve public goodwill toward the sport.

Ethics in Breeding and Competition

Ethical practices are at the heart of pigeon racing. They ensure the sport remains respected and enjoyable for all participants, while safeguarding the well-being of the birds.

1. **Humane Breeding Practices**: Responsible breeders prioritize the health and well-being of their pigeons over producing large numbers of offspring. Avoiding inbreeding and providing proper care for squabs are fundamental to ethical breeding.

2. **Fair Play in Competitions**: Integrity is a cornerstone of pigeon racing. Participants must refrain from unethical behaviors, such as tampering with timing devices, using performance-enhancing substances, or interfering with other racers' birds.

3. **Promoting Bird Welfare**: Overtraining, overcrowding, or racing pigeons under extreme conditions can cause unnecessary stress and harm. Ethical fanciers prioritize their pigeons' health, even if it means withdrawing from a race.

4. **Transparency in Transactions**: Whether buying or selling pigeons, honesty about a bird's lineage, health, and performance history is critical. This fosters trust and credibility within the community.

Navigating Disputes

Disputes are inevitable in competitive sports, and pigeon racing is no exception. Knowing how to handle conflicts professionally and constructively is key to maintaining harmony within the community.

1. **Competition Disputes**: Disagreements over race results, timing errors, or rule violations should be addressed through the proper channels, such as race committees or arbitration panels. Clear evidence and respectful communication often lead to fair resolutions.

2. **Breeding Agreements**: Conflicts can arise when breeders collaborate or sell pigeons. Written contracts outlining expectations, rights, and responsibilities help prevent misunderstandings and provide a basis for resolution if disputes occur.

3. **Mediation and Arbitration**: Many pigeon racing clubs and associations offer mediation services to resolve disputes amicably. Seeking guidance from impartial third parties can help de-escalate tensions and foster mutual understanding.

4. **Building Community Trust**: Upholding ethical standards and respecting others'

rights builds a culture of trust. By prioritizing sportsmanship and fairness, disputes can often be avoided altogether.

Legal and ethical considerations are integral to the longevity and reputation of pigeon racing. By adhering to regulations, practicing humane breeding, and fostering fairness in competition, fanciers can uphold the values that make this sport truly special.

Navigating disputes with professionalism and respect ensures that the community remains united and strong. Whether you're racing for the thrill or breeding for excellence, embracing these principles will help you contribute positively to the sport while protecting its future for generations to come.

CHAPTER SEVENTEEN

INNOVATIONS AND TECHNOLOGY IN PIGEON RACING

The age-old sport of pigeon racing has embraced modern technology, blending tradition with innovation to create exciting possibilities for the future. From advanced tracking systems to sophisticated data analysis tools, these advancements are redefining the way fanciers train, race, and care for their pigeons. In this chapter, we explore the cutting-edge trends, tools, and techniques that are shaping the present and future of pigeon racing.

Emerging Trends in Racing Technology

1. **GPS Trackers**:
   One of the most revolutionary innovations in pigeon racing is the use of GPS trackers. These devices, small enough to be carried by the pigeons, provide real-time data on flight paths, speeds, and distances. This information helps fanciers understand their birds' behavior during races and identify potential areas for improvement.

2. **Genetic Testing for Breeding**:
   Genetic testing is rapidly becoming a game-changer in selecting pigeons with superior racing traits. By analyzing DNA markers, breeders can identify pigeons with strong endurance, speed, and homing abilities, improving the likelihood of producing champions.

3. **Performance-Enhancing Gear**:
   Innovations like aerodynamic bands, lightweight leg rings, and optimized feed containers have entered the market, offering subtle advantages to racing pigeons.

While these tools can enhance performance, their use must align with ethical standards and regulations.

4. **Automated** **Lofts**:
   Modern loft designs now include automated feeding and cleaning systems, reducing manual labor and ensuring consistent care. Some lofts are also equipped with temperature and humidity controls to create an ideal environment for the birds.

Using Data Analytics

The influx of technology in pigeon racing has made data analytics an essential tool for improving performance.

1. **Analyzing** **Race** **Results**:
   By examining historical race data, fanciers can identify patterns in their pigeons' performance, such as strengths in specific weather conditions or routes. This insight helps tailor training programs and select races where their birds are most likely to excel.

2. **Training** **Data** **Monitoring**:
   Tracking training flights with electronic systems allows fanciers to evaluate progress over time. Metrics like average speed, altitude, and homing times provide a detailed picture of a pigeon's readiness for competition.

3. **Predictive** **Analytics**:
   Advanced software programs use machine learning to predict race outcomes based on a bird's past performance, weather conditions, and other variables. These tools give fanciers a competitive edge when planning their strategies.

4. **Benchmarking Against Peers**:
   With access to community databases, fanciers can compare their pigeons' performance against those of other racers, helping identify areas where they need to improve or innovate.

The Future of Pigeon Racing

1. **Artificial Intelligence in Training**:
   AI-powered systems could soon analyze pigeon behavior, optimizing training regimens and even predicting health issues before they arise. This technology has the potential to revolutionize how pigeons are prepared for races.

2. **Virtual Competitions**:
   As technology advances, virtual pigeon racing leagues may emerge, allowing fanciers to compete globally without transporting their birds. GPS trackers and race simulators could make this concept a reality, offering a more inclusive and sustainable way to participate in the sport.

3. **Sustainability Innovations**:
   Future advancements may focus on making pigeon racing more environmentally friendly, with innovations in eco-friendly loft materials, renewable energy solutions for automated systems, and sustainable feed production methods.

4. **Expanded Genetic Research**:
   As genetic technology evolves, breeders may gain deeper insights into the genes that influence racing performance. Ethical considerations will remain critical as the sport navigates these new frontiers.

5. **Global** **Connectivity**:
   The rise of online platforms and social media has already transformed how pigeon fanciers share knowledge and connect. In the future, global virtual communities may play an even greater role in shaping the sport, enabling collaboration and innovation on an unprecedented scale.

Technology is propelling pigeon racing into a new era, offering tools and insights that were once unimaginable. These innovations not only enhance performance but also bring greater understanding and appreciation to the sport.

As we embrace these advancements, it is essential to balance progress with the core values of pigeon racing: respect for the birds, ethical practices, and sportsmanship. By leveraging technology responsibly, the sport can continue to thrive, captivating new generations of fanciers and maintaining its place as a cherished global tradition.

CHAPTER EIGHTEEN

MANAGING A PIGEON RACING TEAM

As your pigeon racing endeavors grow, managing a team becomes increasingly important for achieving success. Whether you're working with partners, building a network, or scaling up your operation, effective team management is crucial. This chapter explores how to collaborate with others, expand your resources, and transition from a hobbyist to a professional racer.

Working with Partners or Assistants

Managing a pigeon racing loft is a demanding task, and collaborating with others can significantly ease the workload.

1. **Defining Roles and Responsibilities**: Clearly outlining the duties of each team member ensures smooth operations. For example, one person might handle feeding schedules, while another focuses on training regimens. Clear communication is key to avoiding overlaps or misunderstandings.

2. **Establishing Trust and Accountability**: Trust is vital in any partnership. Whether working with a partner or hiring assistants, ensure they share your commitment to the welfare of the birds and the integrity of the sport. Regular check-ins and transparent communication build accountability within the team.

3. **Effective Delegation**: Delegating tasks like loft maintenance, health monitoring, or record-keeping allows you to focus on strategy and long-term goals. Equip your assistants

with the knowledge and tools needed to perform their tasks effectively.

4. **Conflict Resolution**: Disagreements can arise in any partnership. Address conflicts promptly and professionally, focusing on solutions rather than assigning blame. This approach preserves the harmony and productivity of the team.

Building a Breeding and Training Network

No pigeon racer is an island. Building a network of fellow enthusiasts can offer invaluable resources, knowledge, and support.

1. **Connecting with Other Breeders**: Establishing relationships with other breeders allows you to exchange birds, diversify your loft's genetics, and learn from their expertise. Attending pigeon racing events, joining clubs, and participating in online forums are excellent ways to build these connections.

2. **Collaborating for Training**: Coordinating training sessions with other racers can expose your birds to new challenges and environments, helping them adapt and improve. Joint releases or shared training routes can benefit all involved.

3. **Participating in Cooperative Breeding**: Collaborative breeding programs enable fanciers to pool their resources and expertise to produce top-quality pigeons. Agreements on shared ownership or breeding rights should be clearly outlined to avoid disputes.

4. **Learning from Experts**: Seek mentorship from seasoned breeders and racers who have a track record of success. Their guidance can accelerate your growth in the sport and help you avoid common pitfalls.

Scaling Your Operation

Transitioning from a casual pigeon racer to a professional requires careful planning and strategic investments.

1. **Evaluating Your Readiness**: Scaling up involves increased responsibilities and expenses. Assess whether you have the time, resources, and commitment needed to manage a larger operation effectively.

2. **Expanding Your Loft**: As your team grows, your loft must accommodate more pigeons while maintaining high standards of care. Plan for additional space, improved ventilation, and more efficient systems for feeding and cleaning.

3. **Hiring Additional Staff**: For large-scale operations, hiring skilled staff becomes necessary. Look for individuals with experience in pigeon care and racing, and provide thorough training to align them with your methods and standards.

4. **Investing in Advanced Tools**: Professional pigeon racers often use advanced equipment like electronic timing systems, GPS trackers, and automated loft systems. These tools enhance efficiency and provide valuable data for improving performance.

5. **Building Your Brand**: As a professional, your reputation is a significant asset. Participate actively in competitions, maintain ethical practices, and share your knowledge with the community. A strong brand can open opportunities for sponsorships, sales, and partnerships.

Managing a pigeon racing team involves more than just caring for the birds—it's about fostering collaboration, building a supportive network, and strategically scaling your operation. With the right team and resources, you can elevate your pigeon racing endeavors from a rewarding hobby to a professional pursuit.

By cultivating partnerships, leveraging community connections, and investing in growth, you not only enhance your chances of success but also contribute to the thriving global community of pigeon racing.

CHAPTER NINETEEN

PSYCHOLOGICAL ASPECTS OF PIGEON RACING

Pigeon racing is as much about understanding the mental and emotional dynamics of the sport as it is about physical preparation. The psychological aspects—both for the pigeons and their owners—play a pivotal role in achieving consistent success. This chapter explores the bond between fancier and bird, stress management techniques, and the importance of patience and consistency in training.

The Bond Between Owner and Bird

The relationship between a fancier and their pigeons is built on mutual trust, care, and understanding. This emotional connection not only enhances the pigeons' performance but also enriches the overall racing experience for the owner.

1. **Understanding Your Pigeons' Behavior**: Observing your pigeons closely helps you recognize their unique personalities, preferences, and habits. Understanding these traits allows you to tailor training and care to their specific needs.

2. **Trust as a Foundation**: Pigeons that trust their owners are more likely to respond positively during training and races. Regular interaction, consistent feeding schedules, and gentle handling foster this trust.

3. **Motivation Through Bonding**: Pigeons are highly intelligent and capable of forming strong bonds with their handlers. This connection can motivate them to return home quickly during races, as they associate home with safety and care.

4. **Emotional   Fulfillment**:
    For many pigeon racers, the bond with their birds goes beyond competition. The mutual respect and affection shared with these animals offer a sense of fulfillment and joy that enhances the entire racing experience.

Stress Management for Pigeons

Stress can negatively impact a pigeon's performance and health. Learning how to minimize stress during various stages of their journey is essential for maintaining their well-being.

1. **Travel   Stress**:
    Long-distance transport to race locations can be stressful for pigeons. Ensuring comfortable, well-ventilated transport cages and minimizing handling during transit helps keep them calm.

2. **Acclimatization**:
    Allowing pigeons time to adjust to new environments, such as race locations, reduces anxiety. Gradual exposure to unfamiliar settings during training also helps them adapt more easily.

3. **Calm   Handling   Practices**:
    Gentle and predictable handling prevents pigeons from associating human interaction with fear. Avoid sudden movements or loud noises when working with your birds.

4. **Pre-Race   Preparation**:
    Providing a calm and quiet environment in the days leading up to a race is crucial. Overexertion or overcrowding can elevate stress levels, so ensure your loft is a sanctuary of peace and routine.

5. **Recovery** **Post-Race**:
   After a race, pigeons need time to recuperate both physically and mentally. Providing them with adequate rest, proper nutrition, and a familiar environment aids in their recovery.

The Role of Patience and Consistency

In pigeon racing, patience and consistency are the keys to success. Building trust and developing skills in your birds takes time, and a steady approach ensures long-term results.

1. **Training** **Progression**:
   Rushing training can overwhelm pigeons, leading to stress and decreased performance. Start with short flights and gradually increase distances to build their confidence and endurance.

2. **Consistency** **in** **Routine**:
   Pigeons thrive on routine. Feeding, training, and cleaning schedules should remain consistent to create a sense of stability for the birds.

3. **Resilience** **Through** **Setbacks**:
   Not every race will result in a win, and not every pigeon will perform as expected. Maintaining patience during setbacks allows you to learn, adapt, and grow as a fancier.

4. **Positive** **Reinforcement**:
   Rewarding pigeons with treats or extra care after a successful training session strengthens their motivation and trust. Positive reinforcement fosters a cooperative relationship between the bird and its owner.

5. **Long-Term** **Vision**:
    Pigeon racing is a journey, not a sprint. Fanciers who focus on gradual improvements and long-term goals often find greater success and satisfaction than those seeking immediate results.

The psychological aspects of pigeon racing emphasize the importance of the emotional connection between fanciers and their birds. By nurturing trust, minimizing stress, and practicing patience and consistency, owners can create an environment where their pigeons thrive.

This chapter reminds us that pigeon racing is more than just a sport—it's a partnership. The success of this partnership hinges on understanding, respect, and a shared journey of growth and achievement. By fostering these psychological elements, you set the stage for both personal satisfaction and competitive success in the rewarding world of pigeon racing.

CHAPTER TWENTY

ENVIRONMENTAL FACTORS AND PIGEON RACING

In pigeon racing, environmental factors are crucial to understanding how pigeons perform and how to adapt training and management strategies for success. From weather conditions to the unique characteristics of urban and rural settings, fanciers must account for many variables. This chapter explores the impact of different environmental conditions, how to adapt pigeon racing strategies accordingly, and the importance of sustainability in the sport.

Impact of Weather Conditions

Weather can significantly influence the performance and well-being of racing pigeons. Extreme weather conditions, whether hot, cold, or rainy, demand specific approaches to training and racing.

1. **Temperature and Flight Performance** Pigeons are sensitive to extreme temperatures, both heat and cold. High temperatures can cause dehydration and fatigue, while cold weather may slow down their metabolism.

   o **Hot Weather**: During summer months, it's vital to train early in the morning or later in the evening when temperatures are cooler. Providing ample shade, clean water, and high-energy food is essential for hydration and stamina.

   o **Cold Weather**: In colder months, pigeons should be gradually acclimatized to the chill.

Keeping lofts well-ventilated but insulated from harsh winds ensures comfort without compromising health. Training should be adjusted to avoid overexertion when temperatures are too low.

2. **Wind and Rain**
Wind and rain can be particularly challenging for pigeon racing, as they directly affect the birds' flight patterns and stamina.

   - **Wind**: Strong winds can either be an advantage or disadvantage, depending on the direction. Headwinds slow pigeons down, while tailwinds can speed up their return. Racing strategies need to consider these factors, possibly adjusting release points or timing to maximize bird performance.

   - **Rain**: Rain can reduce visibility, dampen feathers, and cause fatigue. Pigeons need to be trained to handle wet conditions, and races should be postponed or canceled in heavy rain to ensure the birds' safety.

3. **Training for Various Climates**
Adapting training schedules to match the changing seasons and local climate is key. Pigeons trained in extreme conditions are better prepared to handle the unpredictable nature of race day weather. Regular exposure to variable weather conditions helps build resilience and adaptability in the birds.

Adapting to Urban or Rural Environments

The setting in which pigeons are raised, trained, and raced can dramatically affect their performance. Whether in urban or rural environments, each setting presents unique challenges and opportunities for fanciers.

1. **Urban** **Environments**

   In urban areas, pigeons are often raised and trained in more confined spaces, with limited access to natural landscapes. The noise, buildings, and traffic can introduce additional stress factors.

   - **Loft Management**: Urban lofts may need to be strategically located on rooftops or in quiet courtyards to minimize disturbance. Good ventilation and protection from pollutants are crucial for pigeon health.

   - **Training in the City**: Pigeons trained in the city must adjust to the constant noise and distraction. Training in these conditions requires patience, as pigeons must learn to navigate around obstacles and deal with the stresses of city life.

   - **Urban Adaptations**: Urban racers may have to be more creative in their training methods, using rooftop or park training locations that simulate race-day scenarios.

2. **Rural** **Environments**

   Rural environments offer more space and natural conditions for pigeons to train. These areas often provide an ideal environment for loft management and bird health.

- **Loft Management**: Rural lofts are typically built in open areas with fewer distractions. The layout of the loft is often designed to encourage natural behaviors such as flying and foraging.

- **Training in the Country**: The natural landscape, with its wide open skies and vast horizons, provides an excellent backdrop for training. Long-distance training becomes easier in rural environments due to the lack of obstacles.

- **Advantages of Rural Areas**: With fewer distractions, pigeons trained in rural environments often perform better in natural weather conditions. There is also a greater opportunity to develop larger breeding and racing operations.

Sustainability in Pigeon Racing

As awareness of environmental issues increases, so too does the need for sustainable practices in every aspect of life—including pigeon racing. Eco-friendly methods not only promote long-term environmental health but can also contribute to better pigeon care and performance.

1. **Eco-Friendly Loft Design**
   Sustainable loft design focuses on minimizing waste, energy use, and environmental impact.

   - **Energy Efficiency**: Incorporating natural ventilation, using solar panels for lighting, and using recycled materials can make lofts more energy-efficient. Well-designed lofts reduce the need for heating and cooling, providing a comfortable environment for pigeons with less environmental impact.

- o **Sustainable Building Materials**: Choosing sustainable materials like reclaimed wood or eco-friendly insulation helps reduce the carbon footprint of pigeon racing operations.

2. **Waste   Management**
Proper waste disposal is crucial for the health of the pigeons and the environment.

- o **Waste Disposal**: Pigeon droppings can be composted and used as fertilizer, helping to close the loop on waste and reduce the need for chemical fertilizers. Additionally, waste management systems should be in place to keep lofts clean, minimizing the risk of disease and keeping the birds healthy.

- o **Sustainable Feeding**: Choosing high-quality, locally sourced feed can reduce transportation costs and environmental impact. Feed can also be selected to minimize food waste by providing the right balance of nutrition.

3. **Sustainable Practices for Breeding and Racing**
Fanciers can adopt sustainable practices in breeding and racing to ensure the long-term health of the sport and the environment.

- o **Selective Breeding for Health**: Focus on breeding pigeons with strong immune systems and resilience to disease. This reduces the need for medication and veterinary care, lowering the overall environmental impact.

- o **Promoting Eco-Friendly Brands**: Supporting environmentally responsible brands and suppliers can help ensure that all aspects of the pigeon racing industry are aligned with sustainability efforts.

The environmental factors in pigeon racing—whether related to weather, setting, or sustainability—are interconnected elements that directly influence both the pigeons' performance and the overall success of the sport. By understanding and adapting to these variables, fanciers can create optimal training conditions, manage lofts more efficiently, and embrace eco-friendly practices that support the future of pigeon racing. In doing so, not only will pigeon racing continue to thrive, but it will also do so in a way that is responsible, sustainable, and mindful of the planet.

CHAPTER TWENTY-ONE

STORIES AND ANECDOTES FROM SUCCESSFUL RACERS

The world of pigeon racing is rich with history, innovation, and passion. The success of a pigeon racer is often not just about knowledge and practice, but also about the experiences, challenges, and lessons learned along the way. In this chapter, we'll dive into the stories and anecdotes from the world's top pigeon racers. These insights are a testament to the dedication, perseverance, and love that drive this remarkable sport.

Lessons from Legends

The best pigeon racers often have decades of experience, and their stories are filled with valuable lessons that every aspiring racer can learn from. These legends not only possess expert knowledge but also a deep respect for the birds, the sport, and the community that surrounds it.

1. **Mastering the Basics**

   Top racers often emphasize the importance of mastering the basics before trying to push boundaries. A consistent and disciplined approach to training, breeding, and care forms the foundation of long-term success. Legends in the sport frequently highlight that their journey started with a focus on building solid fundamentals—whether it's daily loft maintenance, understanding pigeons' natural behavior, or perfecting training routines. It's not always about winning; it's about creating a stable, healthy environment for the birds, and success will follow.

2. **Patience and Observation**
   As legendary racers often remind us, patience is key. The sport of pigeon racing isn't just about pushing pigeons to their limits; it's about observation and understanding the birds' unique needs. Some of the greatest successes in the sport have come from racers who took the time to really observe their pigeons' behavior, paying attention to how they recover from training, how they handle different weather conditions, and how their temperament affects race performance. These racers are masters of reading their pigeons, and their patience in waiting for the right moment to train or race is a crucial element of their success.

3. **Innovating While Respecting Tradition**
   While the sport of pigeon racing has a long tradition, successful racers are always looking for ways to innovate. Some of the most influential figures in pigeon racing have blended traditional methods with modern technology. For instance, the use of GPS trackers and electronic timing systems has revolutionized the sport. The legends of the sport understand that while new technology can aid in racing, it should never replace the deep understanding of the birds themselves.

Inspirational Racing Tales

Pigeon racing is a sport filled with remarkable stories of triumph and resilience. Some pigeons have overcome the most difficult odds to achieve greatness, leaving their fanciers with memories and lessons that last a lifetime.

1. **The Resilient Champion**
   One of the most inspirational tales comes from a

pigeon that defied all expectations to win a prestigious race. This pigeon, a humble bird raised by a novice fancier, was often overlooked by others. However, its quiet strength and perseverance led to an incredible comeback. After being released in an area far from its home due to a race mishap, the pigeon struggled for days but managed to find its way back, winning the race despite the odds. This victory became a symbol of hope and resilience for many in the pigeon racing community, showing that even the most unlikely candidates can become champions.

2. **The Underdog's Triumph**
Another unforgettable story involves a pigeon that faced what many thought was a certain defeat. Trained under challenging conditions, this bird had limited resources and minimal support, yet it won race after race. The fancier behind the bird's success shared that the bird's victory was rooted in its determination, similar to the fancier's own struggle to make it in the competitive world of pigeon racing. This story reminds us that while equipment and resources can play a role, the true strength lies in the connection between the fancier and the bird—and their shared commitment to success.

3. **Overcoming Injury to Win**
Injuries are inevitable in the world of pigeon racing, but there are also inspiring stories of pigeons recovering from serious injuries and going on to become champions. One such bird had been struck by a predator and was left with significant damage to its wing. After a period of rehabilitation and care, it

returned to the loft, stronger than ever. The fancier dedicated time to gentle exercises and a tailored recovery plan, gradually helping the bird regain its strength. The bird's ultimate return to racing success was a remarkable feat of both animal resilience and human determination, reminding us that recovery is often part of the journey to greatness.

Personal Experiences

Building a successful racing loft is a journey filled with challenges and victories. Every fancier has their own story of how they got started, the mistakes they've made, and the triumphs they've achieved.

1. **Starting from Scratch**
   Many successful racers began with little more than a passion for pigeons and a strong desire to learn. One fancier shared how they started with only a few birds and a small loft, gradually learning the intricacies of pigeon care, training, and racing. Over time, their loft grew, but so did their knowledge. The process of trial and error, mistakes, and eventual successes was what made the journey so rewarding. These racers emphasize that while it may be overwhelming at first, the key is to stay dedicated and never stop learning.

2. **The Power of Community**
   A common theme in many personal stories is the role of community. Pigeon racing is often seen as a solitary pursuit, but many successful racers attribute their accomplishments to the support of mentors, fellow fanciers, and local racing clubs. One fancier noted how a supportive group of racers helped them through tough times when they were struggling to

train their birds effectively. The exchange of ideas, the sharing of knowledge, and the encouragement from others in the sport made all the difference in their development as a pigeon racer.

3. **The   Joy   of   Success**
Ultimately, the greatest reward for many fanciers comes from the success of their birds. The bond between a fancier and their pigeon is deep and special, and there is no greater satisfaction than watching a bird perform at its peak after months of hard work and care. Whether it's winning a local race or seeing a bird achieve its personal best, the journey of building a racing loft and refining a bird's skills is one of the most fulfilling experiences for any fancier.

The world of pigeon racing is filled with lessons from those who have come before us—stories of persistence, innovation, and triumph. By learning from the legends, drawing inspiration from overcoming obstacles, and reflecting on the personal experiences of fellow fanciers, we can enrich our own journeys in the sport. The stories shared in this chapter show us that pigeon racing is not just about competition; it's about passion, dedication, and the bond between fancier and bird. The successes and challenges along the way are what truly define the sport, making every victory, no matter how small, a testament to the love and commitment that go into it.

CHAPTER TWENTY-TWO

CULTURAL AND GLOBAL PERSPECTIVES ON PIGEON RACING

Pigeon racing is a universal sport with deep roots in various cultures around the world. It transcends borders and brings together enthusiasts from different backgrounds, all united by their love for the birds and the thrill of competition. In this chapter, we explore how pigeon racing differs across countries and cultures, the unique breeds and styles that characterize these regions, and the international competitions that celebrate this fascinating sport on a global scale.

Pigeon Racing Around the World

The sport of pigeon racing is practiced on every continent, each region bringing its unique flavor and traditions to the activity. While the basic principles remain the same—training and racing homing pigeons—local customs and preferences often shape how the sport is conducted.

1. **Europe: The Birthplace of Modern Racing**
   Europe, particularly Belgium and the Netherlands, is considered the heart of modern pigeon racing. These countries have a long history of breeding and training elite racing pigeons. The infrastructure for pigeon racing in Europe is well-established, with numerous clubs, leagues, and a rich culture of camaraderie among fanciers. Belgian and Dutch pigeons are renowned worldwide for their speed and endurance, and the region has produced some of the most prestigious races, such as the Barcelona International.

2. **Asia: Rapid Growth and Enthusiasm**
Pigeon racing in Asia has grown tremendously in recent years, especially in countries like China, Taiwan, and the Philippines. The sport is not only a popular pastime but also a lucrative industry in these regions, with high-stakes competitions offering substantial prize money. In China, pigeon racing has become a status symbol among the wealthy, leading to significant investments in breeding and training programs. Meanwhile, the Philippines is known for its passionate community of racers and its challenging long-distance races across the archipelago.

3. **North America: A Blend of Tradition and Innovation**
In the United States and Canada, pigeon racing has a dedicated following, with clubs and associations actively promoting the sport. The focus often lies on blending traditional methods with modern technology, such as electronic timing systems and data analytics. The North American pigeon racing community values both the competitive and recreational aspects of the sport, making it accessible to a wide range of participants.

4. **Africa: A Growing Tradition**
South Africa, in particular, has emerged as a significant hub for pigeon racing, hosting one of the most prestigious global events, the Million Dollar Pigeon Race. The country's unique climate and geography present distinct challenges and opportunities for racers. South African fanciers have

developed innovative techniques to train pigeons for endurance and resilience.

5. **Australia and New Zealand: Island Challenges**
   In Oceania, pigeon racing thrives despite the challenges posed by the region's isolated geography. Australian and New Zealand racers focus on long-distance and endurance races, often training their birds to navigate vast expanses of ocean. The dedication of fanciers in these regions highlights their commitment to overcoming environmental obstacles.

Unique Breeds and Styles

Different regions have developed unique breeds and styles of racing pigeons, often influenced by local climates, terrains, and preferences.

1. **Belgian   and   Dutch   Pigeons**
   Known for their unmatched speed and stamina, Belgian and Dutch pigeons are often the gold standard in international competitions. These birds are meticulously bred for generations, combining traits that enhance their racing abilities.

2. **Chinese   Breeds**
   In China, there is a growing interest in breeding pigeons specifically for high-stakes competitions. Chinese racers often prioritize traits like sharp homing instincts and adaptability to urban environments.

3. **Philippine   "Balikbayan"   Pigeons**
   The Philippines is famous for its unique approach to pigeon racing, where birds are trained to return home from distant locations across the sea. Breeds here are

valued for their endurance and ability to withstand tropical climates.

4. **South African Endurance Pigeons**
South African pigeons are bred for their ability to endure extreme heat and long distances, making them ideal for the country's demanding races.

5. **American Rollers**
While not exclusively used for racing, roller pigeons in North America highlight the diversity of the pigeon fancier community. These birds, prized for their acrobatic skills, showcase the creative and multifaceted nature of pigeon breeding.

International Competitions and Events

Pigeon racing is not just a local activity—it is celebrated globally through prestigious competitions and events that draw participants from all corners of the world.

1. **The Million Dollar Pigeon Race**
Held in South Africa, this race is one of the most renowned events in the pigeon racing world. It attracts fanciers from across the globe, offering significant prize money and the chance to compete on an international stage. The race tests the pigeons' endurance and ability to adapt to challenging conditions.

2. **Barcelona International**
This iconic European race is a true test of stamina and skill, with pigeons flying long distances across varied terrains. The Barcelona International is considered a hallmark of excellence in the pigeon racing community.

3. **Taiwan's Grand Races**
   Taiwan hosts some of the most competitive pigeon races in Asia, with a focus on speed and precision. These events often feature large purses and showcase the best of Asian breeding and training techniques.

4. **The American Grand National**
   In the United States, the Grand National is a premier event that brings together the best racers from across the country. It emphasizes both the competitive and social aspects of the sport.

5. **Philippine National Races**
   With its challenging routes over land and sea, the Philippine National Races highlight the resilience of both fanciers and their pigeons. These events are a source of national pride and a celebration of the country's vibrant racing culture.

Pigeon racing is a sport that unites people from diverse cultures and backgrounds, each bringing their unique traditions and innovations to the table. Whether it's the precision breeding of Belgian racers, the high-stakes competitions of Asia, or the endurance-focused training in Africa, every region contributes to the richness of the sport. International competitions not only foster a spirit of friendly rivalry but also serve as a platform for fanciers to learn from each other and celebrate their shared passion.

By understanding and appreciating these global perspectives, racers can broaden their horizons, embrace new ideas, and strengthen their connection to the global pigeon racing community. The sport's future lies in this collaborative spirit, where fanciers from around the world come together to celebrate their love for these extraordinary birds.

CHAPTER TWENTY-THREE

ADDITIONAL APPENDICES

The appendices provide invaluable tools and resources designed to enhance your journey in pigeon racing. Whether you're a beginner just starting out or an experienced fancier looking to refine your practices, these supplementary materials aim to simplify complex processes and support your efforts. Below, each section is expanded to provide maximum clarity and utility.

Sample Training Schedules

Training is at the heart of pigeon racing. Having a structured plan ensures consistency and enables you to track progress effectively. Below are sample schedules designed for various stages of a pigeon's development:

1. **Young Pigeon Training Schedule**

    - **Week 1:** Introduce pigeons to their loft surroundings; short, supervised free flights.

    - **Week 2:** Gradually increase the distance of training tosses, starting at half a mile.

    - **Week 3:** Build up to five miles, ensuring birds are confident with their homing abilities.

    - **Week 4:** Introduce team flying to encourage group navigation skills.

Intermediate Training for Active Racers

    - **Early Week:** Conduct morning and evening short-distance tosses (10–15 miles).

- o **Midweek:** Increase distances to 20–30 miles and assess timing accuracy.

- o **Late Week:** Include one long-distance toss (50+ miles) to simulate race conditions.

2. **Pre-Race Conditioning Schedule**

- o **Two Weeks Prior to Race:**

  - Focus on speed drills with shorter distances (5–10 miles).

  - Introduce recovery days with light flying to prevent overtraining.

- o **Final Week:**

  - Include one full-distance trial to mimic race conditions.

  - Ensure rest days to optimize health and stamina.

These schedules are templates you can adjust based on your pigeons' individual needs and responses.

Printable Record-Keeping Templates

Record-keeping is a cornerstone of effective pigeon management. Accurate records allow you to identify trends, evaluate progress, and make informed decisions about breeding, training, and care. Below are descriptions of templates you can use:

1. **Performance Tracker**

- o **Columns:** Bird ID, Training Date, Distance (miles), Flight Time, Speed (mph), Notes.

  o Use this template to monitor improvements in speed and endurance.

2. **Health and Wellness Log**

   o **Columns:** Bird ID, Check-Up Date, Observations (e.g., weight, feathers, appetite), Vet Recommendations.

   o Maintain this log to detect health issues early and track treatments.

3. **Breeding Record**

   o **Columns:** Parent IDs, Date of Mating, Number of Eggs, Hatch Date, Chick ID, Traits Observed.

   o Keep detailed records to ensure the selective breeding of high-performance birds.

These printable templates are designed for ease of use and can be customized to suit your specific management style.

Pigeon Genetics Guide

Understanding pigeon genetics is essential for successful selective breeding. By learning the basics of inheritance, you can predict traits and make informed decisions to develop your flock.

1. **Key Genetic Concepts**

   o **Dominant and Recessive Traits:** Dominant traits (e.g., specific feather patterns) are expressed when one copy of the gene is present, while recessive traits require two copies.

o **Homozygous vs. Heterozygous:** A homozygous bird carries two identical copies of a gene, while a heterozygous bird has one dominant and one recessive gene.

2. **Selective Breeding for Performance**

   o Focus on pairing birds with complementary strengths, such as endurance, speed, or strong homing instincts.

   o Maintain genetic diversity to avoid health complications associated with inbreeding.

3. **Predicting   Outcomes**
   Use a simple Punnett square to anticipate the traits of offspring based on parent genetics. For instance, if two pigeons both carry a recessive gene for a specific feather color, there's a 25% chance their offspring will express that trait.

This guide is designed to empower you with the knowledge to make strategic breeding decisions.

Emergency Care Checklist

In the unpredictable world of pigeon racing, being prepared for emergencies is crucial. This checklist provides step-by-step guidance to handle common injuries and illnesses effectively.

1. **General Supplies to Keep on Hand**

   o Antiseptic solution for cleaning wounds.

   o Bandages and tape for immobilizing injuries.

   o Electrolyte solution for hydration recovery.

- Antibiotics (as prescribed by a veterinarian) for treating infections.

2. **Steps for Common Issues**

   - **Injuries (e.g., Cuts and Bruises):**

     1. Clean the affected area with antiseptic.

     2. Apply a sterile bandage.

     3. Monitor for signs of infection, such as redness or swelling.

   - **Respiratory Distress:**

     1. Isolate the bird from the flock to prevent the spread of illness.

     2. Provide a warm, ventilated space for recovery.

     3. Administer prescribed antibiotics and track progress.

   - **Fatigue or Heat Stress:**

     1. Offer cool water with added electrolytes.

     2. Reduce activity and allow the bird time to rest in a shaded area.

3. **When to Seek Veterinary Assistance**

   - If symptoms persist beyond 48 hours or worsen despite intervention, consult an avian specialist immediately.

This checklist ensures you're well-prepared to provide immediate care and improve your birds' chances of recovery.

The appendices serve as an indispensable companion for pigeon racers of all levels. With practical training schedules, efficient record-keeping templates, a clear genetics guide, and a robust emergency care checklist, these tools equip you with the knowledge and confidence to handle any aspect of pigeon racing. By using these resources, you can streamline your operations, enhance the welfare of your pigeons, and ultimately achieve greater success in the sport.

CHAPTER TWENTY-FOUR

BUILDING A COMMUNITY AROUND PIGEON RACING

A thriving community is the heart of pigeon racing. Engaging with fellow enthusiasts fosters a sense of camaraderie, offers opportunities to learn from others, and helps to share the passion for this timeless sport. Whether connecting online or in person, building and contributing to a supportive community enriches the experience of pigeon racing and ensures its legacy continues.

Joining Pigeon Racing Forums and Groups

In today's digital age, forums and social media groups have become powerful tools for connecting with like-minded individuals. Here's how to leverage these platforms effectively:

1. **Finding the Right Groups**

   - **Online Forums:** Platforms like specialized pigeon racing websites and hobbyist forums are treasure troves of information. Look for forums with active discussions, diverse membership, and reputable moderators.

   - **Social Media Groups:** Facebook, Reddit, and other platforms host dedicated groups where members share tips, race updates, and even live stream events. Search for groups tailored to your region or specific interests in pigeon racing.

2. **Benefits of Online Communities**

   o **Knowledge Sharing:** Forums and groups are ideal for asking questions, sharing experiences, and learning from seasoned racers.

   o **Networking:** Building relationships with fellow enthusiasts can lead to opportunities for mentorship, bird exchanges, or collaboration in breeding programs.

   o **Global Perspective:** Online groups often include members from around the world, providing insights into different techniques, breeds, and racing cultures.

3. **Tips for Engagement**

   o Be an active participant by asking questions, contributing advice, or sharing updates about your loft and races.

   o Respect group rules and foster a positive environment by avoiding conflicts and encouraging constructive discussions.

Hosting Local Pigeon Events

Organizing community events is an excellent way to bring pigeon racing enthusiasts together, promote the sport, and build lasting relationships. Whether it's a small gathering or a larger event, here's how to get started:

1. **Types of Events to Host**

   o **Local Races:** Set up informal races with clear guidelines to encourage participation from nearby racers.

- o **Educational Workshops:** Host sessions on topics like pigeon care, training, or breeding to attract beginners and experienced fanciers alike.

- o **Meetups:** Simple social gatherings can foster a sense of community and allow participants to share stories, tips, and advice.

2. **Steps to Plan a Successful Event**

- o **Choose a Venue:** Find a location that is accessible and appropriate for the event size, such as a local park, community center, or farm.

- o **Spread the Word:** Use flyers, social media, and local pigeon racing clubs to advertise your event.

- o **Engage Attendees:** Plan interactive activities, such as loft tours, Q&A sessions, or prize giveaways, to make the event enjoyable and informative.

3. **The Impact of Local Events**

- o Events help create a strong sense of belonging and encourage participation in the sport.

- o They provide a platform for racers to showcase their birds and share their expertise.

- o By promoting pigeon racing locally, these events can attract new enthusiasts, including younger generations.

Mentorship Opportunities

Mentorship plays a critical role in preserving the art and science of pigeon racing. Whether you are seeking guidance or sharing your expertise, mentorship is a mutually rewarding experience that benefits both mentor and mentee.

1. **Becoming a Mentor**

   o **Share Your Knowledge:** Experienced fanciers can pass on valuable insights into training techniques, breeding programs, and race preparation.

   o **Provide Hands-On Guidance:** Invite mentees to your loft to observe and learn practical skills, from feeding routines to health assessments.

   o **Encourage Growth:** Offer constructive feedback and celebrate their successes, fostering confidence and a love for the sport.

2. **Finding a Mentor**

   o **Join Local Clubs:** Many clubs have experienced members willing to guide newcomers.

   o **Reach Out Online:** Online forums and groups often have mentorship programs or opportunities to connect with experts in the field.

   o **Participate in Events:** Attending races and workshops can lead to meaningful connections with seasoned pigeon racers.

3. **The Value of Mentorship**

- o Mentorship strengthens the pigeon racing community by ensuring knowledge and traditions are passed down to future generations.

- o It provides beginners with a supportive network and a quicker learning curve.

- o Mentors gain fulfillment from sharing their passion and seeing their mentees succeed.

Building a community around pigeon racing creates a rich and rewarding experience for everyone involved. By participating in online forums, hosting local events, and embracing mentorship, you not only deepen your connection to the sport but also contribute to its growth and sustainability. A strong, engaged community ensures that pigeon racing remains a vibrant and cherished tradition for generations to come.

CHAPTER TWENTY-FIVE

CUSTOMIZING LOFT EQUIPMENT

A well-equipped loft is the foundation of a successful pigeon racing operation. Customizing your loft with advanced features, creative DIY projects, and inspiration from global innovations can enhance your pigeons' well-being, streamline management tasks, and improve their overall performance. This chapter explores the potential of personalized loft setups and the tools that can take your loft to the next level.

Advanced Loft Automation

Incorporating automation into your loft can save time, improve consistency in care, and provide optimal conditions for your birds. Modern technology offers solutions for several key aspects of loft management:

1. **Automated Feeding Systems**

   - **How It Works:** Automated feeders dispense measured amounts of food at scheduled times, ensuring your pigeons receive consistent nutrition without overfeeding.

   - **Benefits:** Reduces manual labor, minimizes waste, and promotes a stable feeding routine crucial for racing performance.

   - **Installation Tips:** Choose a system compatible with your loft size and pigeon population, and test it thoroughly to prevent malfunctions.

2. **Climate Control Systems**

    o   **Purpose:** Maintaining an ideal temperature and humidity level is vital for pigeon health, particularly during extreme weather conditions.

    o   **Features:** Systems can include automated ventilation, heating, and cooling to adapt to seasonal changes.

    o   **Additional Benefits:** Proper climate control reduces the risk of respiratory issues and keeps the loft environment stress-free for the pigeons.

3. **Smart Lighting**

    o   **Functionality:** Automated lighting mimics natural daylight cycles, promoting healthy sleep patterns and breeding behaviors.

    o   **Adjustability:** Some systems allow customization to increase light exposure during training seasons or reduce stress in recovery periods.

DIY Loft Projects

For those who enjoy hands-on work, creating custom loft features can be both cost-effective and rewarding. Here are some practical DIY ideas:

1. **Feeding Stations and Drinkers**

    o   **Customized Designs:** Build feeding and watering stations tailored to the size and layout of your loft.

- o **Materials:** Use durable, easy-to-clean materials like stainless steel or plastic to ensure hygiene.

- o **Efficiency:** Incorporate features like spill-proof edges or partitions to reduce waste.

2. **Perches and Nest Boxes**

- o **Perches:** Design multi-level or wall-mounted perches to maximize space and minimize crowding.

- o **Nest Boxes:** Create secure, comfortable boxes with removable panels for easy cleaning and monitoring.

- o **Personal Touch:** Add labels or colors to help identify individual birds' spaces.

3. **Ventilation Solutions**

- o **DIY Ventilation:** Install adjustable vents or fans to improve airflow, especially in compact lofts.

- o **Natural Methods:** Use screened windows or louvers to allow fresh air circulation while keeping predators out.

4. **Waste Management Systems**

- o **Drop Trays:** Build removable trays beneath perches for efficient cleaning.

- o **Composting Units:** Convert pigeon droppings into compost for garden use, promoting sustainability.

Loft Innovations from Around the World

The global pigeon racing community has inspired remarkable loft designs and innovations. Here are some noteworthy examples:

1. **High-Tech Lofts**

   - In countries like the Netherlands and Belgium, racers use lofts equipped with GPS tracking, real-time health monitoring systems, and automated entry traps. .

   - These lofts prioritize precision and data-driven care to optimize racing performance.

2. **Space-Saving Designs**

   - Urban pigeon fanciers in densely populated cities often construct vertical lofts or compact rooftop setups. These designs maximize limited space while maintaining functionality.

3. **Eco-Friendly Lofts**

   - In regions emphasizing sustainability, some lofts integrate solar panels for energy, rainwater collection systems for drinking water, and green roofs for insulation and aesthetics.

4. **Aesthetic Masterpieces**

   - In places like Japan and South Korea, lofts are often designed with artistic touches, blending functionality with architectural beauty. These setups reflect the cultural importance placed on harmony and precision.

Customizing your loft equipment allows you to create an environment tailored to the needs of your pigeons while aligning with your management style and goals. Whether you invest in advanced automation, explore creative DIY projects, or draw inspiration from global innovations, a well-designed loft enhances efficiency and sets the stage for success in pigeon racing. With thoughtful planning and a focus on both practicality and pigeon welfare, your loft can become a model of excellence in the racing community.

CHAPTER TWENTY-SIX

BEHAVIORAL SCIENCE IN RACING PIGEONS

Understanding the behavioral science behind pigeons is crucial for anyone aiming to excel in pigeon racing. By delving into pigeon psychology, employing effective training methods like positive reinforcement, and addressing behavioral issues early, fanciers can foster stronger connections with their birds and achieve better racing outcomes. This chapter explores the science of pigeon behavior, offering practical insights and techniques for managing and optimizing their performance.

Understanding Pigeon Psychology

Pigeons are intelligent and instinct-driven creatures with unique behavioral traits that influence their training and racing performance. By understanding how pigeons think, learn, and respond to their environment, fanciers can tailor their strategies for success.

1. **Natural Instincts**

    o **Homing Ability:** Pigeons have an extraordinary sense of direction, relying on environmental cues such as magnetic fields, the sun's position, and landmarks.

    o **Social Structure:** Pigeons thrive in groups and develop a strong bond with their flock and loft. Understanding their social dynamics can help in training and reducing stress.

2. **Learning Patterns**

    o   **Repetition and Familiarity:** Pigeons learn best through consistent routines, which build familiarity and reduce anxiety.

    o   **Sensitivity to Stimuli:** They respond well to visual and auditory cues, making these tools valuable in training and communication.

3. **Emotional Responses**

    o   **Stress and Anxiety:** Changes in the environment, overtraining, or poor loft conditions can cause stress, impacting performance.

    o   **Confidence Building:** Gradual exposure to new challenges fosters confidence and resilience in racing scenarios.

Training Through Positive Reinforcement

Positive reinforcement is a proven technique for shaping desired behaviors in pigeons. By rewarding good behavior, fanciers can build trust and motivate their birds effectively.

1. **The Role of Rewards**

    o   **Food as Motivation:** Small treats, such as seeds or favorite grains, can be used to encourage desired behaviors like returning to the loft promptly.

    o   **Timing Matters:** Delivering rewards immediately after the desired behavior reinforces the connection between the action and the reward.

2. **Step-by-Step Training**

   - **Gradual Progression:** Start with simple tasks, such as returning to the loft, and gradually introduce more complex challenges like distance flying.

   - **Consistency:** Repetition of training routines at regular intervals ensures pigeons understand and remember the desired behavior.

3. **Building Trust**

   - **Handling and Interaction:** Regular, gentle handling helps pigeons become comfortable with their fancier, reducing fear and fostering a sense of security.

   - **Encouragement:** Use calm, reassuring tones and gestures to establish a positive association with training sessions.

Recognizing Behavioral Issues

Behavioral challenges can hinder training and racing performance. Identifying and addressing these issues early is essential to maintain a healthy and productive loft.

1. **Reluctance to Fly**

   - **Potential Causes:** Fear, illness, or lack of confidence may lead to pigeons avoiding flight.

   - **Solutions:** Provide a safe, stress-free environment, and reintroduce training gradually with plenty of encouragement and rewards.

2. **Loft Loyalty Problems**

   - **Behavior:** Pigeons may struggle to bond with their home loft, especially if relocated.

   - **Strategies:** Encourage loyalty by feeding pigeons exclusively at the loft and maintaining a consistent routine to create a sense of belonging.

3. **Aggression or Social Issues**

   - **Challenges:** Dominant pigeons may bully others, leading to stress and poor performance.

   - **Management:** Monitor loft dynamics and separate aggressive birds if necessary. Introduce perches and nesting areas that minimize competition.

4. **Fear of New Environments**

   - **Indicators:** Hesitation or distress during transport or in unfamiliar locations.

   - **Overcoming Fear:** Gradual exposure to new settings during training builds adaptability and reduces stress during races.

Behavioral science offers valuable insights into the minds and actions of racing pigeons. By understanding their psychology, employing positive reinforcement, and addressing behavioral challenges with patience and care, fanciers can create a supportive and effective environment for their birds. Mastering these principles not only improves racing outcomes but also strengthens the bond between pigeons and their fancier, creating a rewarding and harmonious partnership.

CHAPTER TWENTY-SEVEN

EMERGENCY PREPAREDNESS FOR PIGEON RACERS

Pigeon racing comes with its unique set of challenges, and emergencies can arise unexpectedly. Being prepared to handle threats like predators, natural disasters, or health crises is crucial for protecting the welfare of your pigeons and maintaining a successful loft. This chapter provides comprehensive guidance on dealing with emergencies, from predator management and disaster recovery to assembling an essential first aid kit.

Dealing with Predators

Predators pose a significant threat to pigeons, especially during training sessions or while they are housed in the loft. Effective strategies can minimize these risks and keep your pigeons safe.

1. **Common Predators**

   - **Hawks and Birds of Prey:** Pigeons are natural targets for raptors, particularly during flight training.

   - **Cats and Other Land Predators:** Stray cats, raccoons, and other animals may attempt to access the loft.

2. **Preventative Measures**

   - **Secure Loft Design:** Use strong, predator-proof materials such as wire mesh with small gaps to prevent intrusions.

   - **Flight Training Safety:** Train pigeons during times of lower predator activity, such as early morning or late afternoon, and avoid areas known for hawk sightings.

- o **Deterrents:** Install motion-activated lights, decoys, or reflective objects to discourage predators from approaching the loft.

3. **Responding to an Attack**

- o **Immediate Action:** If a predator is spotted near your pigeons, scare it away using loud noises or water sprays.

- o **Post-Attack Care:** Inspect all pigeons for injuries and address their physical and emotional stress with proper treatment and rest.

Disaster Recovery

Natural disasters or unexpected events can disrupt your loft operations and endanger your pigeons. Preparing for these scenarios ensures a quicker recovery and less stress for both fanciers and their birds.

1. **Common Disasters**

- o **Storms and Extreme Weather:** High winds, heavy rain, or snow can damage lofts and disorient pigeons during flights.

- o **Loft Fires:** Fires caused by electrical faults or nearby hazards can destroy lofts and harm pigeons.

- o **Escapes:** Pigeons may become lost during training or when a loft door is accidentally left open.

2. **Preparation Tips**

   o **Weatherproofing the Loft:** Secure the structure with reinforced materials and ensure proper drainage to withstand storms.

   o **Fire Prevention:** Regularly inspect wiring and install smoke detectors in or near the loft.

   o **Escape Prevention:** Double-check that loft doors and windows are secure, and consider adding a secondary barrier like a vestibule.

3. **Emergency Plans**

   o **Evacuation Kits:** Prepare a portable kit with food, water, and temporary housing in case you need to relocate your pigeons.

   o **Tracking Lost Pigeons:** Ensure all birds are banded with identification details, and notify local pigeon clubs or online forums if a pigeon goes missing.

First Aid Kit for Racing Pigeons

A well-stocked first aid kit can save lives and prevent minor injuries from escalating into serious health issues. Here's what every pigeon fancier should include:

1. **Essential Medical Supplies**

   o **Antiseptics:** For cleaning wounds and preventing infections (e.g., iodine solution).

   o **Bandages and Gauze:** To cover and protect injuries.

- o **Scissors and Tweezers:** For cutting bandages or removing debris from wounds.

2. **Medications and Supplements**

- o **Electrolyte Solutions:** To rehydrate pigeons after stress or illness.

- o **Pain Relievers:** Use pigeon-safe options prescribed by a vet.

- o **Antibiotics:** Keep broad-spectrum antibiotics on hand for emergencies, with proper veterinary guidance.

3. **Specialty Tools**

- o **Splints:** For stabilizing broken or sprained wings and legs.

- o **Syringes:** For administering fluids or medication.

- o **Magnifying Glass:** Useful for inspecting small injuries or signs of parasites.

4. **Storage and Maintenance**

- o Keep the kit in a dry, accessible location near the loft.

- o Regularly check supplies for expiration dates and replace them as needed.

Emergency preparedness is an essential part of pigeon racing. By proactively addressing the risks posed by predators, disasters, and health emergencies, you can safeguard your pigeons and minimize disruptions to your racing operations. A secure loft, a comprehensive first aid kit, and a well-thought-out disaster plan will ensure that both you and your pigeons are ready to face any challenge with confidence.

CHAPTER TWENTY-EIGHT

MARKETING YOUR PIGEON RACING SKILLS

Pigeon racing is not just a sport; it can also be a rewarding business if marketed effectively. Whether you are building your reputation as a breeder, selling pigeons online, or branding your loft, a strong marketing strategy can significantly enhance your success. This chapter offers insights into establishing yourself as a reputable figure in the racing community, leveraging online platforms for sales, and creating a memorable brand identity for your loft.

Building a Reputation as a Breeder or Racer

Your reputation is your most valuable asset in pigeon racing. A history of success, ethical practices, and quality pigeons can open doors to buyers, sponsors, and partnerships.

Leveraging Wins and Pedigrees

- **Showcase Race Success:** Document your wins in local and international races with photos, certificates, and detailed race reports. Share these on social media and community platforms.

- **Highlight Pedigrees:** Maintain detailed records of your pigeons' lineage. Buyers are often willing to pay a premium for birds with proven bloodlines.

- **Participate in Community Events:** Attend pigeon racing expos, club meetings, and other gatherings to network and share your achievements.

Word-of-Mouth Referrals

- **Build Trust:** Deliver quality pigeons and consistently offer valuable advice to your customers. Happy clients are your best marketers.

- **Engage in Mentorship:** Guiding new racers not only strengthens your reputation but also fosters long-term relationships.

Selling Pigeons Online

The internet has revolutionized the way breeders and racers connect with potential buyers. Online platforms provide access to a global audience, making it easier to market and sell racing pigeons.

Platforms for Online Sales

- **Dedicated Pigeon Websites:** Platforms like PigeonAuctions or specialized forums cater to pigeon enthusiasts and are ideal for reaching a targeted audience.

- **Social Media:** Use platforms like Facebook groups, Instagram, and YouTube to showcase your pigeons, share training tips, and engage with the community.

- **E-Commerce Sites:** Websites like eBay or your own online store can be used to sell pigeons, supplies, or training materials.

Tips for Effective Online Advertising

- **High-Quality Photos and Videos:** Clear images and videos showcasing the health, physique, and behavior of your pigeons attract serious buyers.

- **Detailed Descriptions:** Include information on the bird's age, pedigree, racing history, and any awards or achievements.

- **Responsive Communication:** Promptly answer inquiries, and provide additional information or videos upon request to build trust with potential buyers.

Branding Your Loft

Creating a distinct and recognizable identity for your loft sets you apart from competitors and helps establish long-term credibility.

Crafting a Unique Identity

- **Choose a Memorable Name:** Select a name that reflects your loft's values or history. A strong name resonates with the racing community.

- **Design a Logo:** A professional logo adds credibility to your operations and can be used on social media, advertisements, and merchandise.

- **Develop a Motto or Tagline:** A catchy phrase that encapsulates your loft's mission can leave a lasting impression.

Building an Online Presence

- **Create a Website:** A dedicated website showcasing your pigeons, race results, and breeding services gives potential buyers a professional first impression.

- **Blog or Vlog Content:** Sharing insights about pigeon care, training, and racing techniques establishes you as an authority in the field.

- **Social Media Engagement:** Post regularly on platforms like Instagram, Facebook, and TikTok to connect with pigeon racing enthusiasts and promote your services.

Merchandise and Memorabilia

- **Sell Loft-Branded Products:** T-shirts, caps, or mugs with your loft's name and logo can create additional revenue and increase brand visibility.

- **Offer Pigeon Racing Guides:** If you've developed expertise, consider creating and selling training manuals, e-books, or video tutorials under your brand.

Marketing your pigeon racing skills is about more than just selling pigeons; it's about establishing a presence in the community and fostering long-term relationships. By building a reputation for quality and professionalism, utilizing online platforms effectively, and branding your loft, you can attract buyers, sponsors, and collaborators. With a thoughtful marketing approach, you can elevate both your standing in the sport and the success of your pigeon racing operations.

CHAPTER TWENTY-NINE

YOUNG PIGEON RACER'S GUIDE

Pigeon racing is a rewarding and dynamic sport that can be enjoyed by people of all ages. Encouraging young enthusiasts to join the racing community not only ensures the future of the sport but also provides valuable lessons in responsibility, patience, and sportsmanship. This chapter explores ways to engage youth in pigeon racing, the opportunities available through youth-oriented competitions, and how pigeon racing can foster family bonding.

Engaging Youth in Pigeon Racing

Introducing children and teenagers to pigeon racing can be a transformative experience, helping them develop a sense of responsibility and connection to animals while learning valuable life skills.

Starting Young

- **Education through Experience:** Start by teaching children about the birds themselves—explaining their anatomy, behavior, and history. Kids are naturally curious, and fostering that curiosity is a great way to spark interest.

- **Hands-On Learning:** Let young enthusiasts take part in daily tasks like feeding, cleaning, and even training pigeons. These hands-on activities foster a deeper connection to the birds and a sense of ownership.

- **Incorporating Technology:** Many youth enjoy technology, so introducing them to apps or devices used in modern pigeon racing (like GPS trackers) can make the sport more appealing and help them engage with it in a way they find exciting.

Mentorship

- **Building Relationships with Experienced Racers:** Pairing youth with experienced mentors helps them learn the finer points of the sport. It also gives young racers someone to look up to, encouraging them to stick with the hobby and learn from others.

- **Encouraging Peer Groups:** Foster a community for young racers to share their experiences and learn together. Online forums or local clubs can help create a social aspect around pigeon racing that young enthusiasts will find motivating.

Youth-Oriented Competitions

Competitions provide young racers with tangible goals to work toward, along with the excitement of friendly rivalry. Many pigeon racing organizations offer events designed specifically for younger participants, which are an excellent way to motivate and inspire them.

Junior Leagues

- **Junior Competitions:** Many pigeon racing clubs have junior leagues where young participants can enter races without the pressure of competing with seasoned racers. These leagues often have shorter, less challenging race distances, ensuring the experience remains fun and educational.

- **Supportive Environment:** Youth competitions often foster a supportive environment where younger racers can receive guidance and encouragement from more experienced competitors. This camaraderie can inspire confidence and develop leadership skills.

Youth-Friendly Events

- **Annual Youth Races:** Several major racing organizations host special races for young fanciers. These races typically come with reduced entry fees and prizes aimed at encouraging long-term participation.

- **Skills Workshops:** Look for events that offer workshops specifically designed for younger racers. These might include hands-on training sessions, classes on pigeon care, or seminars on how to manage race day logistics.

Family Bonding Through Pigeon Racing

Pigeon racing is a wonderful activity for families to enjoy together. The sport offers opportunities for shared experiences, teamwork, and learning, all of which can help strengthen family bonds.

Shared Responsibilities

- **Involving Everyone in Loft Management:** Family members can work together to clean the loft, prepare food, and maintain equipment. Assigning roles and responsibilities helps foster teamwork, allowing the entire family to contribute to the care of the pigeons.

- **Training as a Family Activity:** When training pigeons, families can take turns working with the birds. Kids can be involved in tasks such as releasing pigeons for flight training, tracking their progress, or even assisting with training sessions.

Family Competitions and Events

- **Create Family Competitions:** Host informal family races or challenges to keep the excitement alive. You can have a fun competition to see who can train their pigeons to fly the furthest or who can record the best time for a training session.

- **Attend Events Together:** Participating in pigeon racing events as a family—whether locally or at national championships—can create lasting memories. These experiences not only foster excitement but also provide opportunities for learning and networking with other families involved in the sport.

Teaching Life Lessons

- **Responsibility and Commitment:** Pigeon racing teaches kids valuable lessons in responsibility. They'll learn the importance of regular care routines, respect for animals, and the dedication required to succeed in the sport.

- **Sportsmanship and Respect:** Through competitions, children learn how to handle success and failure graciously. They understand that the race is about more than just winning—it's about the journey, the care they give to their birds, and the friendships they build along the way.

Pigeon racing offers young enthusiasts a unique opportunity to connect with nature, develop responsibility, and enjoy a fun and rewarding sport. By encouraging youth involvement, providing opportunities for youth-oriented competitions, and promoting family participation, we ensure that pigeon racing remains a thriving, multi-generational sport. Whether it's through mentoring, friendly competitions, or shared family experiences, pigeon racing can play an integral role in fostering lifelong bonds and creating a community that celebrates both the birds and the people who love them.

CHAPTER THIRTY

HISTORICAL AND CULTURAL SIGNIFICANCE OF PIGEON RACING

Pigeon racing is not just a modern sport; it is deeply intertwined with history, culture, and even warfare. The role of pigeons extends far beyond the racetrack, with significant contributions to human society. This chapter delves into the historical and cultural significance of pigeon racing, examining famous events and pigeons, the pivotal role of pigeons during wartime, and how pigeons have been revered in various cultures and traditions.

Famous Pigeon Races in History

Throughout history, pigeon racing has produced some remarkable moments that have solidified its place in both sport and society. These events and the birds involved have become legends, showcasing the incredible feats that pigeons are capable of achieving.

The First Official Pigeon Race

- **The Birth of Pigeon Racing:** The first official pigeon race took place in 1818 in France. The event involved sending pigeons from Paris to a remote location and then timing their return to the city. This marked the beginning of pigeon racing as a competitive sport, though pigeons had long been used for communication before this formalization.

- **The Rise of the Sport:** Pigeon racing grew rapidly, particularly in Europe, in the 19th century. The sport reached new heights in the early 20th century, with major international competitions like the London National and the Brussels Classic drawing large crowds and showcasing the talents of both pigeons and their handlers.

Legendary Pigeons and Races

- **Cher Ami:** One of the most famous pigeons in history, Cher Ami, became a war hero during World War I. Despite being injured, Cher Ami delivered a crucial message that saved the lives of soldiers, cementing the pigeon's place in history as a symbol of bravery.

- **The Great Race of 1931:** Known as the "Great Race" in Belgium, this event saw pigeons travel over 1,000 kilometers to their home lofts, with the fastest pigeon completing the race in under 12 hours. This race highlighted the stamina and speed of racing pigeons and set the stage for future world records in the sport.

Pigeons in War and Peace

The role of pigeons in wartime is one of the most profound aspects of their historical significance. Beyond their value in racing, pigeons were instrumental in military communications during both World Wars.

Carrier Pigeons in World War I and II

- **Vital Messengers:** During the wars, pigeons were used to carry messages across enemy lines when other forms of communication failed. They were especially useful when radios or wires were destroyed or unreachable. Pigeons like Cher Ami played a pivotal role in saving countless lives by delivering critical intelligence, medical information, or distress signals.

- **The Pigeon Post Service:** In addition to the military use of pigeons, many countries set up official pigeon post services during wartime. These services ensured that vital information could be delivered despite the destruction of traditional communication networks.

Pigeons in Peaceful Times

- **Communication in Remote Areas:** Beyond wartime, pigeons have been used to communicate across vast distances, particularly in isolated regions where other forms of transportation or communication were not feasible. In areas such as the Swiss Alps, pigeons played a key role in relaying messages between remote villages.

- **Symbol of Hope and Freedom:** After the wars, pigeons were often released as a symbol of peace and freedom. They became a living reminder of the sacrifices made and the restoration of peace.

Cultural Symbols and Stories

Pigeons hold significant cultural and symbolic value in many societies, with deep roots in mythology, religion, and folklore. They have been revered as symbols of peace, love, and fidelity, and their portrayal varies widely across cultures.

Pigeons in Religion and Mythology

- **Symbols of Peace:** The most universally recognized cultural symbol of pigeons is their association with peace. This symbolism stems largely from religious traditions, particularly Christianity, where the dove (a type of pigeon) is seen as a symbol of the Holy Spirit and peace. The image of a dove carrying an olive branch has become an enduring emblem of peace worldwide.

- **Hinduism and Ancient Greece:** In Hinduism, the pigeon is associated with the god of love, Kama, and is seen as a symbol of attraction and affection. In ancient Greece, pigeons were revered as messengers of the gods, and their ability to find their way home was seen as a divine quality.

Pigeons in Folklore

- **The Homing Instinct:** Pigeons' extraordinary homing abilities have led to their portrayal in various stories and legends. In many cultures, pigeons are thought to be able to carry messages between the human world and the divine, often acting as intermediaries between gods and mortals.

- **The Role of Pigeons in Local Traditions:** In various parts of the world, pigeons are seen as symbols of love and loyalty. In some cultures, pigeons are kept as pets and are used in ceremonial rituals, such as weddings or religious celebrations, to symbolize the unity of a couple or community.

Pigeons in Literature and Art

- **Artistic Depictions:** Pigeons have long been depicted in art, particularly in European Renaissance paintings where they often symbolized purity, peace, and divine love. The use of pigeons in art continues today, reflecting their enduring cultural importance.

- **Literary Significance:** Pigeons are also featured prominently in literature, often symbolizing freedom, hope, or the spread of ideas. The famous novel *The Pigeon* by Patrick Süskind explores the connection between the protagonist and the bird, using it as a metaphor for isolation and existential anxiety.

Pigeon racing is not merely a competitive sport; it is deeply intertwined with history, culture, and symbolism. From the legendary pigeons that have changed the course of wars to their role in various religious and cultural traditions, pigeons hold a special place in human history. The sport itself, while modern in its form, is part of a long and rich legacy that continues to evolve today. Understanding the historical and cultural significance of pigeon racing provides a deeper appreciation for the birds and the sport, recognizing them not only as athletes but as symbols of resilience, communication, and peace.

CHAPTER THIRTY-ONE

ADVANCED GENETICS AND BREEDING TECHNIQUES

In the world of pigeon racing, genetic factors play a crucial role in the performance and success of the birds. Advanced genetics and breeding techniques allow racers to enhance their pigeons' natural abilities, ensuring they are suited for the challenges of competitive racing. This chapter explores the cutting-edge methods used to select and breed high-performance pigeons, including genetic testing, cloning, and strategies for breeding birds tailored to specific race conditions.

Genetic Testing for Racing Pigeons

In recent years, genetic testing has revolutionized the way breeders approach the selection of their pigeons. With the aid of modern science, breeders can now make more informed decisions about pairing pigeons for optimal performance, health, and longevity.

The Role of Genetic Testing

- **Understanding Inherited Traits:** Genetic testing allows breeders to identify which traits—such as endurance, homing ability, and flight speed—are inherited. By analyzing the genetic makeup of pigeons, breeders can select birds with the best combination of desirable traits, leading to offspring with enhanced racing potential.

- **Health and Disease Resistance:** Genetic testing can also identify susceptibility to certain diseases or health conditions. This enables breeders to avoid pairing birds that may pass on genetic weaknesses, ultimately improving the overall health of the racing flock.

Tools and Techniques for Genetic Testing

- **DNA Profiling:** By analyzing the DNA of pigeons, breeders can gain insights into their genetic lineage and identify specific markers linked to performance traits. DNA testing can also reveal whether a pigeon carries recessive genes that may affect future generations.

- **Genetic Markers for Racing Traits:** Researchers have identified specific genetic markers that correlate with important traits for racing pigeons, such as muscle fiber composition, wing size, and cardiovascular efficiency. Breeding pigeons with these markers can significantly enhance performance in different race conditions.

Benefits of Genetic Testing

- **Improved Predictability:** By utilizing genetic data, breeders can more accurately predict the performance of future generations, reducing the element of guesswork in pigeon breeding.

- **Genetic Diversity:** While selecting for desirable traits is important, genetic testing also helps ensure the genetic diversity of the breeding population, reducing the risk of inbreeding and the associated negative health effects.

Cloning and Genetic Engineering

The future of pigeon breeding is shaped by advances in cloning and genetic engineering, two highly controversial fields in genetics. While these technologies offer the potential to produce pigeons with superior traits, they also raise ethical concerns that must be carefully considered.

Cloning Pigeons

- **How Cloning Works:** Cloning involves creating an identical genetic copy of a pigeon by inserting its DNA into an egg cell, which then develops into a bird genetically identical to the original. Cloning could allow breeders to replicate high-performing pigeons, ensuring the continuation of their successful genetic line.

- **Pros and Cons of Cloning:** While cloning may offer the opportunity to produce top-tier racing pigeons with exceptional traits, it also presents risks. Clones can suffer from health issues, and the lack of genetic diversity could lead to weakened immune systems and increased susceptibility to disease.

Genetic Engineering and Gene Editing

- **CRISPR and Gene Editing:** Technologies like CRISPR allow breeders to edit specific genes in a pigeon's DNA, potentially enhancing desirable traits such as flight speed or endurance. Gene editing could also be used to eliminate genetic diseases or improve the pigeon's ability to handle stress during races.

- **Ethical Considerations:** The use of cloning and gene editing in pigeon racing raises ethical questions. Some argue that it may compromise the natural integrity of the birds, while others believe it could lead to a new era of performance breeding. It is crucial for breeders to approach these technologies with a sense of responsibility, ensuring they are used to enhance the well-being of the birds, not just to create perfect specimens for competition.

Breeding for Specific Race Conditions

One of the most important aspects of advanced pigeon breeding is tailoring pigeons to meet the specific challenges of different types of races. The demands of short, medium, and long-distance races vary, and pigeons must be bred with these conditions in mind.

Breeding for Short-Distance Races

- **Speed and Agility:** Pigeons bred for short-distance races (typically 100 to 300 kilometers) must possess exceptional speed and agility. These races require birds that can reach top speeds quickly and navigate through changing weather conditions and varying landscapes.

- **Breeding Strategy:** To breed pigeons suited for short-distance races, breeders typically focus on selecting birds with strong, muscular builds and excellent cardiovascular health. A shorter, more compact body and a high proportion of fast-twitch muscle fibers help these pigeons achieve high-speed bursts.

Breeding for Medium-Distance Races

- **Endurance and Navigation:** Pigeons bred for medium-distance races (300 to 600 kilometers) need a combination of speed and endurance. These races often involve longer flight times, requiring pigeons to maintain consistent energy levels over a sustained period.

- **Breeding Strategy:** Pigeons for these races are selected for their balanced traits, including moderate size, efficient flight muscles, and a high level of endurance. Additionally, breeders focus on pigeons with strong homing instincts and excellent navigation abilities to ensure they can return home over longer distances.

Breeding for Long-Distance Races

- **Stamina and Longevity:** For long-distance races (over 600 kilometers), stamina and the ability to cope with extreme physical stress are paramount. These pigeons must be able to fly for hours, sometimes over a full day, without tiring, and endure the elements without compromising performance.

- **Breeding Strategy:** Long-distance racing pigeons are typically bred for their larger size and slower-twitch muscle fibers, which support extended flight. Breeders often select pigeons that exhibit exceptional recovery rates and the ability to handle adverse weather conditions, such as wind or rain.

Adapting to Changing Conditions

- **Selective Breeding for Weather and Terrain:** In addition to focusing on distance and stamina, breeders must also consider environmental factors such as weather and terrain. For example, pigeons bred for races in hot climates must be able to handle extreme heat, while those racing in mountainous regions need to be strong climbers. Breeding pigeons for these specific conditions ensures that they perform optimally, regardless of external challenges.

Advanced genetics and breeding techniques are transforming the future of pigeon racing. By using genetic testing to select optimal breeding pairs, employing cutting-edge technologies like cloning and gene editing, and tailoring pigeons for specific race conditions, breeders can enhance the performance, health, and longevity of their racing birds. However, with these powerful tools come ethical responsibilities. As the sport evolves, it is crucial for breeders to balance innovation with care, ensuring the well-being of the birds remains a priority. The future of pigeon racing lies in this delicate harmony between science and tradition, leading to stronger, more capable pigeons that continue to soar to new heights.

CHAPTER THIRTY-TWO

MOTIVATION AND GOAL SETTING FOR RACERS

Success in pigeon racing doesn't happen overnight. It requires a combination of dedication, strategic planning, and a strong mental attitude. Setting clear, realistic goals, staying motivated in the face of setbacks, and drawing inspiration from others are essential components of a successful racing career. This chapter will provide insight into how to set achievable goals, overcome challenges, and stay inspired to keep pushing forward, even when the going gets tough.

Setting Realistic Goals

One of the most important steps in pigeon racing is setting goals that are challenging yet achievable. Whether you're just starting out or looking to improve your performance, having a clear set of objectives will help you stay focused and motivated.

Start with Small, Attainable Goals

For new racers, it can be tempting to aim for top positions right away. However, it's important to set small, incremental goals that allow you to build skills and confidence over time. These goals might include:

- **Learning Loft Management:** Starting with understanding how to care for pigeons, manage their health, and create a conducive racing environment.

- **Mastering Training Routines:** Setting a goal to consistently follow a training schedule for a few weeks to develop a solid foundation for your pigeons.

- **Achieving Personal Bests:** Instead of focusing solely on winning races, aim to improve your birds' performance relative to their previous results.

Set Long-Term and Short-Term Goals

It's essential to balance short-term and long-term goals. Short-term goals keep you motivated on a daily or weekly basis, while long-term goals provide an overarching direction for your pigeon racing journey.

- **Short-Term Goals:** These could include goals such as training your birds for a particular race, improving their flying endurance, or increasing their speed.

- **Long-Term Goals:** Examples include becoming a top competitor in a particular race series, breeding a specific line of high-performing pigeons, or expanding your loft with top-tier breeding pairs.

Be Flexible and Adjust Goals as Needed

Sometimes, despite our best efforts, things don't go according to plan. Whether it's an injury, unforeseen circumstances, or simply a poor race result, it's important to reassess and adjust your goals accordingly. Flexibility allows you to stay on track while adapting to challenges.

Overcoming Setbacks

Setbacks are an inevitable part of pigeon racing. Every racer, no matter how experienced, faces challenges such as poor performance, injuries, or losses. The key to long-term success is learning how to handle these setbacks without losing motivation.

Dealing with Failures

Not every race will be a win, and some races might not go as planned. However, failures are often the best learning opportunities.

- **Analyze the Situation:** After a disappointing performance, take the time to evaluate what went wrong. Was it the weather, the training, or a mistake in loft management? Understanding the root cause allows you to correct it for future races.

- **Learn from Others:** Seek advice from experienced racers who have faced similar setbacks. Their insights can help you avoid common mistakes and speed up your learning curve.

- **Stay Positive:** Remember that setbacks are temporary, and perseverance is key. Use each failure as motivation to improve and strive for better results in the next race.

Handling Injuries

Injuries can sideline both pigeons and racers alike. It's important to approach injuries with patience and care.

- **Give Pigeons Time to Heal:** If a pigeon is injured, give it the time it needs to recover. Rushing recovery can lead to more severe injuries or setbacks.

- **Stay Calm as a Racer:** Injuries can be frustrating, but it's essential to keep a level head. Instead of becoming discouraged, use the downtime to refine other aspects of your racing preparation, such as loft management or training routines.

Managing Unexpected Losses

Occasionally, pigeons might go missing during a race or training session. While this can be emotionally difficult, it's important not to dwell on the loss for too long.

- **Focus on the Future:** Rather than focusing on what you've lost, focus on the birds that remain and the future races you will participate in.

- **Keep Birds Safe:** Ensure that measures are in place to reduce the chances of losses, such as using GPS tracking for long-distance training or securing lofts against predators.

Staying Inspired

In pigeon racing, inspiration often comes from within, but it can also be drawn from others. Staying inspired is vital for long-term success, especially during times of adversity.

Drawing Strength from Top Racers

Many top racers have faced significant challenges and failures before achieving success. Their resilience and ability to keep going despite obstacles serve as powerful examples for others.

- **Stories of Resilience:** For instance, a renowned racer might share how they bounced back after an injury to their prized pigeon or overcame a long losing streak to win a major competition. These stories highlight the importance of persistence, patience, and the ability to learn from mistakes.

- **Mentorship:** Seek out a mentor who can offer advice, encouragement, and share their own experiences. The guidance and support of someone who has been through the highs and lows of the sport can reignite your own passion and inspire you to keep pushing forward.

Staying Motivated Through Small Wins

Celebrate the small victories along the way. Every improvement in your pigeons' performance or a successful training session is a win worth recognizing.

- **Tracking Progress:** Keep a journal or log to track your pigeons' improvements over time. Seeing tangible progress can provide the motivation needed to stay committed to your goals.

- **Rewards:** Treat yourself when you achieve key milestones, whether it's a successful race or a new breeding achievement. These small rewards will keep you inspired and ready for the challenges ahead.

Embrace the Journey

Pigeon racing is as much about the journey as it is about the destination. Enjoy the process of learning, training, and growing alongside your pigeons. Every race and every challenge provide opportunities for personal and professional growth.

- **Focus on the Experience:** Appreciate the joy of working with your birds, the thrill of competition, and the camaraderie of fellow racers. The passion for the sport should always be at the heart of your efforts, regardless of the outcome of individual races.

Pigeon racing, like any competitive sport, requires more than just skill—it demands mental strength, resilience, and the ability to stay motivated through setbacks. By setting realistic goals, learning how to deal with failures, and staying inspired by the stories of others, you can maintain the determination needed to succeed in the long run. Whether you're overcoming challenges or celebrating victories, remember that perseverance is key. The journey of pigeon racing is filled with ups and downs, but with the right mindset, the rewards are well worth the effort.

CHAPTER THIRTY-THREE

ADDITIONAL FEATURES

To provide comprehensive support for both new and seasoned pigeon racers, this chapter offers a variety of additional features designed to enhance your pigeon racing experience. From interactive guides to technological recommendations, these resources aim to simplify complex processes, improve efficiency, and provide valuable insights for achieving success in the sport.

Interactive Resources
Step-by-Step Guide on Loft Construction, Training, and Health Checks

Creating a well-designed loft, establishing an effective training regimen, and ensuring the health of your pigeons are essential components of successful pigeon racing. This guide provides a systematic approach:

1. **Loft Construction**

   o **Choosing the Location:** Select an area with good ventilation, minimal predator access, and protection from extreme weather.

   o **Design and Layout:** Opt for a structure that balances comfort and security, featuring nesting boxes, perches, and adequate spacing to prevent overcrowding.

   o **Material Selection:** Use durable, predator-resistant materials, such as wire mesh with small gaps and sturdy wood or metal framing.

- o **Maintenance Tips:** Schedule regular cleaning and inspections to ensure hygiene and structural integrity.

2. **Training Regimen**

   - o **Gradual Training:** Start with short flights close to the loft and increase distance progressively.

   - o **Route Familiarization:** Train pigeons to recognize local landmarks for better homing accuracy.

   - o **Training Groups:** Work with small groups of pigeons for focused attention and improved results.

   - o **Performance Assessment:** Keep records of flight times, distances, and any challenges encountered during training sessions.

3. **Health Checks**

   - o **Routine Inspections:** Examine pigeons weekly for signs of illness, including feather condition, weight changes, and energy levels.

   - o **Vaccination and Parasite Control:** Follow a schedule for essential vaccinations and administer deworming treatments regularly.

   - o **Veterinary Support:** Partner with a vet experienced in avian care to address health concerns promptly.

This guide serves as a blueprint for establishing and maintaining a successful pigeon racing operation.

Training Plans

Printable and editable training plans help you stay organized and consistent in preparing your pigeons for competition. These plans include:

1. **Daily Training Schedule**

    o Outline specific times for feeding, loft flying, and free-flight training.

    o Include rest periods to prevent overexertion.

2. **Weekly and Monthly Goals**

    o Set milestones for distance, speed, and endurance improvement.

    o Plan recovery days to allow pigeons to regain energy and avoid burnout.

3. **Performance Tracking Templates**

    o Record individual pigeon statistics, such as flight times, weight, and race results.

    o Analyze trends to identify high-performing birds and areas for improvement.

These templates are designed for flexibility, allowing you to customize them to suit your unique goals and strategies.

Mobile App Recommendations

Incorporating technology into pigeon racing management can significantly streamline operations. Below are recommended apps that cater to various aspects of the sport:

1. **Flight and Training Tracking Apps**

   - **Features:** GPS tracking for real-time monitoring of flight paths, speeds, and distances.

   - **Benefits:** Provides data to refine training techniques and improve race performance.

2. **Health and Nutrition Management Apps**

   - **Features:** Record feeding schedules, track weight, and log health observations.

   - **Benefits:** Simplifies monitoring and ensures consistency in care.

3. **Race Management Platforms**

   - **Features:** Access race calendars, registration details, and live updates.

   - **Benefits:** Keeps you informed about upcoming events and competition results.

These tools offer convenience and enhance decision-making through data-driven insights.

Competition Calendar

This sample global pigeon racing schedule highlights key events, ensuring you never miss an opportunity to compete or network with other fanciers:

1. **Major International Races**

   o **South African Million Dollar Pigeon Race:** A prestigious event that attracts competitors worldwide.

   o **Barcelona International Race:** Known for its challenging long-distance course.

2. **Regional Competitions**

   o **National Championships:** Held in various countries, offering opportunities for fanciers to showcase their pigeons locally.

   o **Club Races:** Beginner-friendly events organized by local pigeon clubs.

3. **Registration Tips**

   o **Deadlines:** Mark key dates to avoid late entries.

   o **Preparation Checklist:** Ensure your pigeons meet health and identification requirements for each event.

This calendar is a valuable resource for planning your racing season effectively.

Common Racing Pigeon Breeds

Understanding the unique characteristics of different racing pigeon breeds allows you to select the best birds for your loft.

1. **Popular Breeds**

   - **Janssen:** Renowned for speed and short-distance performance.

   - **Van Loon:** Ideal for long-distance endurance races.

   - **Meuleman:** A balanced breed excelling in various conditions.

2. **Breed Selection Tips**

   - Consider the specific demands of your preferred race distances.

   - Evaluate traits such as wing structure, muscle tone, and adaptability.

3. **Visual Guide**

   - Includes images and descriptions to help identify key physical features.

This guide ensures you make informed breeding and purchase decisions to enhance your loft's competitiveness.

Advanced Health Monitoring Checklist

A structured approach to monitoring pigeon health is essential for maintaining peak performance. This checklist includes:

1. **Weight Management**

   o Weigh pigeons regularly to detect subtle changes that may indicate health issues.

2. **Flight Time Records**

   o Log times consistently to track improvements or identify potential concerns.

3. **Fitness Assessments**

   o Examine wing strength, energy levels, and overall condition before and after races.

4. **Early Warning Signs**

   o Reference a list of symptoms, such as decreased appetite or changes in behavior, to catch illnesses early.

This checklist equips you with the tools needed to ensure your pigeons remain healthy and competitive throughout the season.

The additional features presented in this chapter provide practical, professional resources to support every aspect of pigeon racing. By utilizing step-by-step guides, detailed training plans, advanced tools, and interactive materials, you can elevate your skills and achieve your goals in the sport. These resources empower you to manage your loft effectively, optimize your pigeons' performance, and navigate the competitive world of pigeon racing with confidence.

CHAPTER THIRTY-FOUR

ADVANCED TOPICS FOR EXPERTS

As pigeon racing evolves, expert-level fanciers continually seek ways to refine their strategies and enhance the performance of their birds. This chapter delves into advanced training techniques, focusing on optimizing for diverse environmental conditions and developing mental resilience in pigeons. These topics are designed for racers who aim to compete at the highest levels of the sport.

Advanced Training Techniques
Weather-Based Training

Weather conditions significantly influence the outcome of pigeon races, and advanced fanciers must understand how to prepare their birds to excel under varying circumstances.

1. **Understanding Weather Dynamics**

   o **Wind Patterns:** Train pigeons to fly against headwinds for endurance and with tailwinds to maximize speed. Sidewind training improves their ability to maintain course.

   o **Humidity:** Acclimate pigeons to higher humidity by gradually exposing them to controlled conditions that mimic tropical climates.

   o **Temperature Extremes:**

     - **Heat Training:** Limit training sessions during peak heat to prevent heatstroke but incorporate short flights during warm hours to build tolerance.

- **Cold Weather Preparation:** Focus on energy-dense nutrition and shorter flights to maintain strength during freezing conditions.

2. **Training Adjustments**

   o Analyze weather forecasts before sessions to match conditions with race scenarios.

   o Use simulated conditions, such as wind tunnels or indoor climate controls, to replicate challenging environments.

3. **Post-Training Recovery**

   o Provide electrolyte supplements after sessions in extreme weather to aid hydration and recovery.

   o Monitor behavior for signs of fatigue or heat stress and adjust training intensity accordingly.

Altitude and Terrain Adaptation

Races involving varying elevations and challenging landscapes require pigeons to develop unique physical adaptations and navigational skills.

1. **Altitude Training**

   o Gradually increase training heights by releasing pigeons from elevated locations.

   o Focus on short bursts of high-intensity flights to strengthen their cardiovascular systems and prepare them for reduced oxygen levels at higher altitudes.

o   Monitor recovery times post-flight, ensuring pigeons adapt to thinner air efficiently.

2. **Terrain Familiarization**

o   Train pigeons over diverse landscapes, including valleys, hills, and mountainous areas, to enhance their adaptability.

o   Use marked landmarks in training routes to teach pigeons to navigate natural obstacles effectively.

o   Include water crossings in practice flights to build confidence for coastal or riverine races.

3. **Energy Optimization for Terrain Races**

o   Increase carbohydrate intake before long or steep elevation flights to provide sufficient energy reserves.

o   Use a mix of short and long flights in rugged terrains to develop strength and stamina simultaneously.

Mental Toughness in Pigeons

Racing pigeons face numerous distractions and stressors during competitive events. Developing mental resilience ensures they remain focused and perform optimally.

1. **Building Focus**

o   Train pigeons in environments with mild distractions, such as moderate noise or visible wildlife. Gradually increase exposure to more challenging conditions.

- o Encourage group cohesion by training pigeons to fly in small groups to simulate race-day dynamics.

2. **Stress Management**

- o Minimize handling stress by creating a consistent routine for loft entry, feeding, and release.

- o Introduce gradual exposure to new experiences, such as transportation crates or new release sites, to reduce anxiety during actual races.

3. **Overcoming Fatigue**

- o Use interval training to build endurance and recovery speed during prolonged flights.

- o Provide supplements rich in protein and essential amino acids after intense sessions to aid muscle repair.

4. **Simulating Race-Day Challenges**

- o Conduct mock races with varied distances and multiple release points to mimic real competition scenarios.

- o Use time trials to help pigeons adapt to the pressure of timed performance.

Mastering these advanced techniques allows experienced racers to push their pigeons' capabilities to new heights. By integrating weather-based training, altitude adaptation, and mental toughness exercises into your regimen, you can prepare your birds for the most challenging race conditions.

With a blend of strategic planning, environmental acclimatization, and psychological resilience, your pigeons will be equipped to excel at the highest levels of competition.

Precision Nutrition for Optimal Performance

Nutrition is the cornerstone of a racing pigeon's success. Proper feeding not only ensures robust health but also directly impacts performance, endurance, and recovery. This chapter explores how to fine-tune your pigeons' diet to maximize their potential through seasonal adjustments, custom supplement formulations, and advanced probiotic strategies for optimal gut health.

Seasonal Dietary Adjustments

Racing pigeons have varying nutritional needs throughout the year, depending on the demands of the racing calendar. Tailoring their diet to these changing needs is essential for maintaining peak performance.

Pre-Race Season Nutrition

Before the racing season begins, focus on building your pigeons' strength and endurance:

- **High-Carbohydrate Diets:** Introduce energy-rich grains such as corn and barley to develop energy reserves.

- **Protein for Muscle Building:** Include peas, beans, and lentils to promote muscle growth and recovery.

- **Micronutrients:** Add vitamins A, D, and E to support bone strength, feather quality, and overall vitality.

Race Season Nutrition

During the racing season, your pigeons need a diet that fuels their intense physical activity:

- **Balanced Energy Mix:** Provide a blend of carbohydrates and fats to ensure sustained energy. A mix of safflower seeds, sunflower hearts, and oats works well.

- **Hydration Boosters:** Include electrolytes in drinking water to replace salts lost during flights and prevent dehydration.

- **Quick Recovery Foods:** After races, feed pigeons lighter grains like white rice and milo to replenish glycogen stores.

Post-Race Recovery Diet

Following the race season, the focus shifts to restoring health and preparing for the next cycle:

- **Detoxification Grains:** Offer a diet of easily digestible grains such as wheat and small seeds to give the digestive system a break.

- **Immune System Support:** Add garlic oil and brewer's yeast to boost immunity and overall health.

- **Feather Quality:** Increase omega-3 fatty acids (e.g., flaxseed or fish oil) to enhance feather condition during molting periods.

Custom Supplement Formulas

Each pigeon has unique nutritional needs, influenced by genetics, age, and workload. Crafting personalized supplements can bridge gaps in their diet and give them a competitive edge.

Base Ingredients for Supplement Mixes

1. **Protein Sources:** Soy protein or egg powder for muscle repair.

2. **Energy Boosters:** Honey or maltodextrin for quick-release energy.

3. **Essential Fats:** Omega-3 and omega-6 fatty acids for sustained energy and anti-inflammatory benefits.

Formulation Tips

- Consult a veterinarian or avian nutritionist to determine precise nutrient requirements.

- Adjust formulations weekly based on weather conditions, race difficulty, and recovery rates.

- Avoid over-supplementation, which can lead to digestive issues or nutrient imbalances.

Sample Supplement Recipes

- **Pre-Race Energy Mix:**

  - 50% safflower seeds

  - 20% sunflower hearts

  - 10% honey-coated oats

  - 10% wheat germ oil

  - 10% brewer's yeast

- **Recovery Formula:**
  - 40% split peas
  - 30% rice powder
  - 20% flaxseed oil
  - 10% probiotic powder

Probiotic and Gut Health Management

Gut health plays a pivotal role in a pigeon's digestion, immunity, and endurance. Probiotics help maintain a healthy balance of gut microbiota, which is critical for optimal performance.

Role of Probiotics in Racing Pigeons

- **Improved Digestion:** Probiotics enhance nutrient absorption, ensuring pigeons get maximum energy from their feed.

- **Boosted Immunity:** A healthy gut reduces susceptibility to common illnesses, particularly during the stress of racing.

- **Enhanced Recovery:** Probiotics support faster recovery by reducing inflammation and aiding tissue repair.

Sources of Probiotics

- **Natural Sources:** Yogurt (small amounts), fermented grains, or apple cider vinegar (diluted in water).

- **Commercial Probiotic Supplements:** Opt for high-quality avian-specific probiotics available in powder or liquid forms.

Probiotic Protocol

- **Daily Maintenance:** Add a pinch of probiotic powder to food or water during the off-season.

- **Pre-Race Boost:** Increase the dosage three days before a race to prepare the gut for stress.

- **Post-Race Recovery:** Administer probiotics immediately after races to restore gut balance.

Precision nutrition is essential for unlocking the full potential of your racing pigeons. By implementing seasonal dietary adjustments, formulating custom supplements, and prioritizing gut health through probiotics, you can significantly enhance their performance, resilience, and recovery. Thoughtful attention to their nutritional needs not only gives your pigeons a competitive edge but also ensures their long-term health and well-being.

Race Data Analytics

In the evolving world of pigeon racing, data analytics has become an indispensable tool for gaining a competitive edge. Whether you're refining training methods, strategizing future races, or evaluating your pigeons' potential, leveraging race data provides valuable insights that go beyond instinct and tradition. This chapter explores how to utilize modern tools and techniques for analyzing GPS data, interpreting historical race results, and assessing pigeon potential based on measurable performance indicators.

Using GPS Data for Performance Insights

Modern GPS trackers have revolutionized pigeon racing by providing detailed flight data. By understanding and applying these insights, racers can fine-tune their training routines and optimize performance.

Key Metrics from GPS Data

1. **Flight Paths:** Analyze the routes your pigeons take to identify inefficiencies or deviations. Straight, efficient paths are ideal, while frequent detours may indicate disorientation or fatigue.

2. **Speeds:** Measure average, peak, and sustained speeds to determine a bird's endurance and sprinting capability.

3. **Altitude and Terrain Navigation:** Evaluate how pigeons handle different elevations and challenging terrains, such as hills or valleys.

4. **Rest Stops:** Detect where and how often pigeons stop during flights, which could indicate areas of weakness or external interference.

How to Refine Training Using GPS Insights

- **Route Optimization:** Design training routes that encourage pigeons to take more efficient paths. For example, simulate race conditions by gradually increasing distance and complexity.

- **Target Weaknesses:** If a pigeon struggles with specific terrains or distances, adjust their training to address these challenges.

- **Group Dynamics:** Use GPS to monitor how pigeons perform in groups versus individually. Some birds may excel in solitary flights but underperform in a flock.

Case Study: Training with GPS

A fancier noticed one of his pigeons frequently veered off course during training. By analyzing GPS data, he identified distractions near a specific urban area. Adjusting the training route helped the bird focus and improve its race performance significantly.

Analyzing Historical Race Data

Historical race data is a treasure trove of information that can reveal patterns, highlight strengths, and expose areas for improvement. By systematically analyzing past results, racers can make data-driven decisions for future competitions.

Leveraging Historical Data for Strategy

1. **Trend Analysis:** Study race conditions (e.g., weather, distance, and terrain) to identify trends where your pigeons perform well or struggle.

2. **Competitor Insights:** Evaluate the performance of rival lofts to understand their strengths and weaknesses. This can help you anticipate competition strategies.

3. **Performance Consistency:** Track individual birds' results across multiple races to assess their reliability under varying conditions.

Racing Pigeons Mastery Unleashed

Tools for Analyzing Historical Data

- **Spreadsheets:** Use programs like Excel or Google Sheets to organize and analyze race data.

- **Specialized Software:** Invest in pigeon racing software that offers advanced analytics and visualization tools.

- **Race Records:** Maintain detailed logs of every race, including environmental factors, bird-specific data, and results.

Actionable Insights from Historical Data

- Adjust training intensity during certain seasons if past data shows a drop in performance under extreme heat or cold.

- Select optimal race distances for individual birds based on their previous successes at short, medium, or long distances.

Example: Predicting Success Using Data

A racer analyzed three years of race results and discovered that his loft consistently underperformed in long-distance races during late summer. Adjusting feeding regimens and training schedules helped improve results in subsequent seasons.

Evaluating Pigeon Potential

Traditionally, pigeon evaluation relied heavily on pedigree and instinct. However, data analytics offers a more objective and precise way to assess a bird's potential.

Key Performance Indicators (KPIs) for Evaluation

1. **Consistent Speed:** Birds with stable performance metrics over multiple races often have high potential for reliability.

2. **Recovery Rates:** Fast recovery from races indicates strong health and resilience.

3. **Adaptability:** Assess how pigeons perform under varying conditions, such as different weather patterns or race terrains.

4. **Flight Efficiency:** Evaluate the efficiency of a pigeon's flight path, as it directly affects their energy expenditure.

Combining Data with Pedigree

- While pedigree provides an important foundation, supplementing it with race and training data allows for a more comprehensive evaluation.

- Use GPS trackers and historical race results to identify pigeons that may outperform their lineage expectations.

Data-Driven Selection

- **Training Candidates:** Identify which young pigeons show promise during initial training based on speed, flight path, and recovery metrics.

- **Breeding Decisions:** Select breeders not only based on pedigree but also on proven performance data.

Benefits of Objective Evaluation

- Minimizes emotional bias in decision-making.

- Ensures resources are invested in pigeons with the highest potential for success.

Race data analytics is an essential tool for any modern pigeon racer seeking a competitive edge. By utilizing GPS trackers, analyzing historical race data, and evaluating pigeon potential with measurable metrics, you can refine your strategies, improve training routines, and make informed decisions about breeding and racing. Embracing data-driven techniques not only elevates your loft's performance but also positions you at the forefront of this ever-evolving sport.

Advanced Breeding for Performance

Breeding plays a pivotal role in developing a successful team of racing pigeons. With advancements in genetics and deeper insights into breeding strategies, fanciers can now achieve greater precision and predictability in producing top-performing birds. This chapter delves into advanced breeding techniques such as line breeding and crossbreeding, explores the growing use of artificial insemination, and examines the role of epigenetics in shaping racing traits.

Line Breeding vs. Crossbreeding

Breeding strategies profoundly impact the vigor, predictability, and performance of offspring. Two primary methods, **line breeding** and **crossbreeding**, offer unique advantages and challenges.

Line Breeding: Enhancing Predictability

Line breeding involves mating closely related pigeons, such as siblings, half-siblings, or parents with offspring, to consolidate desirable traits within a bloodline.

Racing Pigeons Mastery Unleashed

Advantages:

- Reinforces specific traits, such as speed, stamina, or homing ability.

- Increases the chances of producing offspring similar to a proven champion.

Challenges:

- Risk of inbreeding depression, where excessive genetic similarity reduces vigor and resilience.

- Requires meticulous record-keeping to avoid unintended weaknesses.

Best Practices:

- Maintain diversity by occasionally introducing unrelated birds to refresh the gene pool.

- Focus on traits critical to your racing goals, ensuring only the strongest performers are included in the breeding program.

Crossbreeding: Balancing Vigor and Performance

Crossbreeding involves pairing pigeons from unrelated bloodlines to introduce genetic diversity and vigor.

Advantages:

- Often produces hybrid vigor (heterosis), resulting in stronger, healthier offspring.

- Allows the combination of complementary traits from different bloodlines, such as speed from one line and endurance from another.

Challenges:

- Outcomes are less predictable compared to line breeding.

- Requires careful selection to ensure desirable traits align in the offspring.

Best Practices:

- Pair birds with complementary strengths to balance the traits of both bloodlines.

- Use crossbred offspring selectively for racing or as a foundation for future breeding.

Artificial Insemination in Racing Pigeons

Artificial insemination (AI) is an advanced technique that allows fanciers to maximize the breeding potential of elite pigeons. While more commonly used in livestock, AI is gaining traction in pigeon racing as a tool for controlled breeding.

How Artificial Insemination Works

1. **Semen Collection:** Semen is collected from a high-performing male pigeon using gentle, specialized techniques.

2. **Preparation:** The semen is evaluated for quality, diluted if necessary, and stored temporarily.

3. **Insemination:** The female pigeon is carefully inseminated using a sterile tool, ensuring precision.

Benefits of Artificial Insemination

- **Selective Breeding:** Enables pairing of pigeons that may not mate naturally due to distance, temperament, or health issues.

- **Maximized Genetics:** A single male can sire multiple offspring in a single breeding season, enhancing his influence on the loft's gene pool.

- **Controlled Outcomes:** Reduces the risk of unintended matings and ensures the intended pair's traits are passed on.

Challenges and Ethical Considerations

- Requires skill and experience to perform effectively without causing stress to the birds.

- May be viewed by some as unnatural or against the spirit of traditional pigeon breeding.

Recommendation: Use AI selectively and responsibly to complement, not replace, natural breeding methods.

Epigenetics in Pigeons

Epigenetics is an emerging field that explores how environmental factors can influence gene expression without altering the DNA sequence itself. In racing pigeons, understanding and leveraging epigenetics can unlock new possibilities for improving performance.

What Is Epigenetics?

Epigenetics refers to modifications that regulate how genes are expressed. These changes can be influenced by factors such as diet, training, stress, and environment.

Key Concepts:

Racing Pigeons Mastery Unleashed

- **Gene Activation and Suppression:** Certain environmental stimuli can "turn on" or "turn off" specific genes.

- **Heritability:** Epigenetic changes can sometimes be passed to offspring, providing a way for acquired traits to influence future generations.

Epigenetics in Pigeon Racing

- **Diet and Nutrition:** Tailored feeding programs can enhance gene expression related to endurance, muscle development, and immunity.

- **Training Regimens:** Consistent and challenging training routines can activate genes associated with stamina and stress resilience.

- **Environmental Factors:** Exposure to varying climates or terrains during training can prepare pigeons for diverse race conditions by influencing adaptive gene expression.

Harnessing Epigenetics for Better Performance

- **Controlled Stress Exposure:** Introduce pigeons to mild stressors, such as simulated race environments, to build resilience without causing harm.

- **Optimal Nutrition:** Incorporate supplements and probiotics that promote gut health, which in turn influences genetic expression related to energy metabolism.

- **Rest and Recovery:** Prioritize rest periods to allow epigenetic adaptations to consolidate, ensuring long-term benefits.

Advanced breeding techniques, when applied thoughtfully, can significantly elevate the performance of a pigeon loft. By balancing line breeding and crossbreeding, utilizing artificial insemination responsibly, and exploring the potential of epigenetics, fanciers can achieve unprecedented success in producing pigeons that excel in speed, stamina, and adaptability. As these methods continue to evolve, they offer exciting possibilities for the future of pigeon racing.

Advanced Loft Management

A well-managed loft is the cornerstone of successful pigeon racing. As the sport evolves, so do the tools and techniques for optimizing loft conditions. Advanced loft management focuses on leveraging technology and innovative practices to ensure pigeons remain healthy, comfortable, and primed for peak performance. This chapter explores climate-controlled lofts, automated tracking systems, and scalable pest and disease prevention strategies for larger operations.

Climate-Controlled Lofts

Maintaining a consistent and optimal environment within the loft is crucial for the health and performance of racing pigeons. Modern technology allows fanciers to regulate temperature, humidity, and air quality with precision.

Why Climate Control Matters

1. **Temperature Regulation:** Extreme temperatures can stress pigeons, affecting their immune system and training capabilities.

2. **Humidity Levels:** High humidity promotes mold growth and respiratory issues, while overly dry conditions can lead to dehydration and feather damage.

3. **Air Quality:** Poor ventilation can lead to a buildup of ammonia and other harmful gases, increasing the risk of respiratory infections.

Technological Solutions for Climate Control

- **Automated Climate Systems:** Install systems that monitor and adjust temperature and humidity automatically. Many modern units come with smartphone connectivity for remote management.

- **Ventilation Upgrades:** High-efficiency fans and air filters can ensure a steady flow of clean air while removing dust and allergens.

- **Heating and Cooling Units:** Use energy-efficient heaters and air conditioning units to maintain optimal temperatures year-round.

Practical Tips

- Position lofts to minimize exposure to direct sun in hot climates or to shield against harsh winds in colder regions.

- Regularly inspect climate-control equipment to ensure consistent performance.

Automated Tracking Systems

Technology has revolutionized how fanciers monitor and manage their pigeons. Automated tracking systems now provide real-time insights into the birds' health, activity levels, and overall well-being.

Racing Pigeons Mastery Unleashed

Benefits of Automated Tracking

1. **Real-Time Monitoring:** Gain immediate updates on pigeon activity, ensuring early detection of issues like illness or reduced mobility.

2. **Improved Training Insights:** Track flight patterns, feeding habits, and time spent on perches to refine training regimens.

3. **Data-Driven Decisions:** Use collected data to identify trends and make informed adjustments to diet, training, and loft management.

Popular Tracking Tools

- **RFID Systems:** Attach RFID chips to leg bands to track individual pigeons as they enter and exit the loft. These systems can also log feeding and exercise habits.

- **GPS Trackers:** Lightweight GPS units provide detailed flight data, including routes, speeds, and altitude, which can inform training programs.

- **Smart Lofts:** Integrate cameras, sensors, and automated feeders to create a fully monitored environment that reduces manual labor while improving oversight.

Implementation Tips

- Choose tracking systems that integrate seamlessly with your existing loft setup.

- Train yourself and any staff on the system to maximize its utility.

- Regularly back up data to analyze long-term trends and outcomes.

Pest and Disease Prevention for Large Operations

For large-scale pigeon racing operations, maintaining loft hygiene and preventing disease becomes a more complex but equally critical task. Scalable solutions are essential to ensure a healthy flock, especially when managing hundreds of pigeons.

Pest Control Strategies

1. **Rodent Management:** Mice and rats can spread disease, consume feed, and damage loft infrastructure.

    o Use sealed feed storage containers to prevent contamination.

    o Install physical barriers, such as mesh screens, to block access points.

    o Deploy traps or non-toxic repellents to keep rodents at bay.

2. **Insect Control:** Flies, mites, and lice can cause discomfort and spread infections among pigeons.

    o Regularly clean and sanitize loft surfaces to reduce breeding grounds.

    o Use safe insecticides or natural repellents to treat affected areas.

- o Implement ultraviolet light traps to minimize fly populations.

Disease Prevention Protocols

- **Vaccination Programs:** Develop a vaccination schedule tailored to your flock's needs, focusing on common diseases such as paramyxovirus and pigeon pox.

- **Quarantine Procedures:** Isolate new or returning pigeons for at least two weeks to monitor for signs of illness before introducing them to the main loft.

- **Regular Health Checks:** Conduct routine inspections of pigeons for signs of illness, such as lethargy, weight loss, or abnormal droppings.

Hygiene Practices for Large Lofts

- Use pressure washers and disinfectants to clean loft surfaces regularly.

- Install automated waterers and feeders to reduce contamination risks.

- Implement a waste management system to remove droppings and other debris efficiently.

Advanced loft management combines innovative technology with practical solutions to create an optimal environment for racing pigeons. By integrating climate control, leveraging automated tracking systems, and implementing scalable pest and disease prevention strategies, fanciers can ensure their pigeons remain in peak condition. As these tools and practices continue to evolve, they promise to enhance both the health and performance of competitive flocks.

International Competition Strategies

Participating in international pigeon racing events is a prestigious milestone for many fanciers. However, competing on a global stage introduces unique challenges that require careful planning and adaptation. From preparing pigeons for new environments to building a global network and managing transportation logistics, this chapter provides a comprehensive guide to excelling in international races.

Preparing Pigeons for Global Races

Adapting pigeons to unfamiliar climates, time zones, and release locations is critical for success in international events. Racing in foreign conditions tests a pigeon's resilience and adaptability, making targeted preparation essential.

Climate Adaptation

1. **Acclimation to Temperature Changes:**

   - Gradually expose pigeons to temperature ranges similar to the race location to minimize stress.

   - Use climate-controlled lofts or outdoor conditioning for controlled exposure.

2. **Humidity and Air Quality:**

   - Familiarize pigeons with environments mimicking the race location's humidity levels.

- o Monitor and maintain respiratory health with supplements that support lung function.

Time Zone Adjustments

- Begin feeding and training schedules that align with the time zone of the race weeks before departure.

- Gradually shift light exposure to mimic sunrise and sunset timings at the destination.

Release Location Familiarization

- Study the terrain, elevation, and possible environmental challenges at the release point.

- When possible, send pigeons to a local partner in the race country for pre-race training to acclimate them to the area.

Networking with Global Breeders and Racers

The pigeon racing community is a vast network of fanciers, breeders, and competitors. Building international connections provides opportunities to share knowledge, gain insights, and foster collaborative relationships.

Building Relationships

1. **Joining Global Associations:**

   - o Become a member of international pigeon racing organizations and forums.

   - o Attend global conferences, exhibitions, and races to meet fellow enthusiasts.

2. **Participating in Online Communities:**

- o Engage in social media groups, forums, and virtual events to discuss strategies and share experiences.

- o Use platforms like YouTube or blogs to showcase your loft's achievements, attracting potential collaborators.

3. **Hosting and Visiting International Fanciers:**

- o Invite foreign breeders to visit your loft and exchange ideas.

- o Travel to other countries to observe loft setups and training methods firsthand.

Knowledge Exchange and Collaboration

- Share insights on genetics, training, and health management with global contacts.

- Partner with breeders abroad for joint ventures in breeding or racing.

- Utilize international networks to source high-quality pigeons for your loft or sell your own.

Logistics of Transporting Pigeons

Ensuring safe and stress-free transport for pigeons to international race locations is vital for their health and performance. Improper handling during travel can lead to stress, fatigue, or illness, significantly affecting race outcomes.

Pre-Travel Preparation

1. **Health Checks and Documentation:**

   o Schedule veterinary checks to ensure pigeons are fit for travel.

   o Obtain required health certificates and vaccination records for the destination country.

2. **Travel Conditioning:**

   o Familiarize pigeons with transport crates to reduce anxiety during the journey.

   o Feed them a light, easily digestible diet before travel to prevent digestive issues.

Choosing the Right Transport Method

- **Air Transport:**

   o Opt for airlines experienced in handling live animals.

   o Use well-ventilated crates designed to minimize movement and keep pigeons calm.

- **Road Transport:**

   o Ensure vehicles are equipped with proper ventilation and temperature control.

   o Schedule breaks to check on the birds and provide hydration if necessary.

Minimizing Stress During Travel

- Use calming supplements or sprays specifically designed for birds during transport.

- Avoid excessive handling or abrupt movements while loading and unloading crates.

Competing in international pigeon racing events requires meticulous preparation and a proactive approach to overcoming challenges. By acclimating pigeons to new environments, fostering a network of global connections, and ensuring stress-free transportation, fanciers can elevate their performance on the global stage. Success in these prestigious events not only showcases the skill and dedication of the racer but also reinforces the universal appeal of pigeon racing as a sport that transcends borders.

The Science of Homing Instincts

Pigeons have long been renowned for their incredible homing abilities, a characteristic that has made them invaluable in racing, messaging, and even military operations. Understanding the science behind their navigation can significantly improve training, health management, and race performance. This chapter explores the cutting-edge research on homing instincts, expert techniques to enhance these abilities, and the potential disruptions that can affect their navigation.

Cutting-Edge Research on Homing Abilities

Pigeons' ability to return home from vast distances is a remarkable phenomenon that has intrigued scientists for centuries. Recent studies have uncovered fascinating details about the mechanisms pigeons use to navigate, which are critical for both racing and survival.

Magnetic Fields and Earth's Magnetic Field

Recent research suggests that pigeons use the Earth's magnetic field to navigate. Special receptors in their beaks, often referred to as "magnetoreceptors," allow them to sense magnetic fields. These receptors help pigeons determine their position relative to their home loft and adjust their flight paths accordingly. This magnetic sense is especially useful when other environmental cues, like visual landmarks, are absent.

- **Key Finding:** Studies have shown that disrupting these magnetic cues can impair the pigeon's ability to navigate properly, particularly over long distances.

Olfactory Cues and Smell

Alongside magnetic fields, pigeons use their sense of smell to guide them back home. Research by scientists like *Gagliardo et al.* in 2019 suggests that pigeons rely heavily on olfactory cues from the environment. The theory is that pigeons memorize specific smells from their loft surroundings and use them to create a "smell map" of their area. When released at a distant location, they can use this olfactory map to guide them back.

- **Key Finding:** Experiments involving blocking pigeons' sense of smell have shown a significant reduction in their ability to return home, confirming that their olfactory sense is a primary navigation tool.

Celestial Positioning

Pigeons also rely on the sun and stars for navigation, a method known as celestial navigation. During the day, they use the position of the sun to determine direction, adjusting for the time of day. At night, they turn to the stars, particularly the North Star, for orientation.

- **Key Finding:** This celestial compass helps pigeons during long flights, particularly when other cues (like magnetic fields or olfactory markers) are unavailable. In fact, pigeons that were kept in environments with limited access to light sources were found to have impaired navigation.

Enhancing Homing Accuracy Through Training

While pigeons possess an inherent homing instinct, training can enhance their ability to navigate more efficiently, especially in racing scenarios. Expert-level techniques focus on strengthening their natural instincts and improving their performance in different environmental conditions.

Gradual Distance Training

One of the most effective training strategies for improving homing accuracy is gradual distance training. This involves releasing pigeons progressively further from their loft, starting from short distances and increasing incrementally. This method allows pigeons to familiarize themselves with longer flight paths and reinforces their ability to return home accurately.

- **Pro Tip:** Start with distances of about 5-10 kilometers, gradually increasing by 10-20 kilometers. Ensure that the pigeons are always capable of returning safely before increasing the distance.

Variable Release Locations

Training pigeons to return home from different locations, rather than just one specific point, enhances their spatial memory and adaptability. Varying the release sites helps pigeons strengthen their reliance on both olfactory cues and magnetic field orientation, encouraging them to use multiple navigation techniques.

- **Pro Tip:** Use various geographic landmarks like rivers or mountains to help pigeons hone their ability to identify different environments. Release pigeons in unfamiliar areas, focusing on diverse environments to prepare them for more complex routes.

Route Repetition and Consistency

Pigeons perform best when they are trained along established routes. Regular practice along the same flight paths helps reinforce their natural homing instinct. By repeating routes, pigeons improve both their speed and efficiency, reducing the time it takes to find their way home.

- **Pro Tip:** Incorporate randomization within the established routes to challenge the pigeons, ensuring that they develop flexibility while maintaining their core navigation skills.

Disruptions to Homing Abilities

While pigeons are remarkable navigators, several environmental or biological factors can disrupt their homing abilities. Understanding these factors is key to maintaining healthy, high-performing birds.

Magnetic Field Disruptions

Pigeons' reliance on Earth's magnetic field can be disrupted by artificial magnetic fields, such as those from power lines, radio towers, or even the metal structures of buildings. These disruptions may confuse pigeons or even cause them to become disoriented.

- **Mitigation:** When training pigeons in urban areas, it's important to monitor the proximity of strong electromagnetic fields. If pigeons struggle with navigation, consider relocating training sessions to areas with fewer artificial influences.

Weather Conditions

Severe weather conditions, including strong winds, heavy rain, and fog, can also affect homing abilities. These elements hinder the pigeons' ability to see landmarks, measure distances, or interpret celestial cues.

- **Mitigation:** Monitor weather forecasts closely and avoid releasing pigeons during inclement weather. In cases where pigeons are already airborne, be prepared to bring them back early or guide them to shelter.

Physical and Health Issues

Pigeons suffering from physical injuries, malnutrition, or illness may experience difficulty navigating, as their energy levels and overall stamina are compromised. A bird's homing ability is closely linked to its physical condition, making health management crucial.

- **Mitigation:** Maintain a rigorous health check routine, ensure optimal nutrition, and provide proper rest to ensure that pigeons are physically capable of performing at their best.

Understanding and enhancing the homing instinct of pigeons requires a combination of cutting-edge scientific knowledge and practical training strategies. From leveraging the latest research on magnetic fields and olfactory cues to employing expert-level techniques that enhance natural instincts, fanciers can optimize their pigeons' ability to navigate. However, environmental disruptions and health factors can pose challenges, so it's vital to regularly monitor both external conditions and the birds' overall well-being. With careful management, pigeons' incredible homing abilities can be harnessed to achieve exceptional performance, whether in competitive racing or long-distance navigation.

Ethics and Sustainability in Pigeon Racing

Pigeon racing, like many sports, has its challenges, not only in terms of the competition but also in maintaining ethical standards and promoting sustainability. This chapter explores how to maintain ethical practices in breeding and racing, implement sustainable strategies for pigeon racing operations, and navigate the complex landscape of regulations and compliance that govern the sport.

Maintaining Ethical Standards in Breeding and Racing

The ethical treatment of pigeons is a vital component of pigeon racing, particularly as the sport evolves and modernizes. Addressing concerns about the well-being of the birds ensures that the practices within the sport are humane, respectful, and responsible.

Overtraining and Exhaustion

Overtraining pigeons can lead to fatigue, injuries, and even long-term health issues. It's essential to monitor training sessions to ensure that pigeons are not being pushed beyond their natural capabilities. Healthy training routines must strike a balance between exertion and recovery to optimize performance without causing harm.

- **Best Practice:** Gradually increase the distance and intensity of training while always giving pigeons ample time to recover. Monitoring their condition after each training session can help detect signs of exhaustion or distress early.

Culling and Welfare Concerns

Culling, or the practice of eliminating pigeons from the breeding program or racing team due to poor performance or other factors, raises ethical concerns. The act of culling must be done responsibly, with a focus on the health and well-being of the bird. There should be alternatives to culling whenever possible, such as retirement to a non-competitive environment or rehoming pigeons for breeding or pet purposes.

- **Best Practice:** Avoid unnecessary culling by considering the broader needs of the pigeon, including its potential in other capacities, and providing proper care. When culling is necessary, ensure it is done humanely and in compliance with animal welfare standards.

Ensuring Overall Welfare

A major ethical consideration in pigeon racing involves the overall well-being of the birds, including their mental and physical health. Training routines should not compromise their health, and adequate nutrition, rest, and medical care must be prioritized at all stages of their involvement in the sport.

- **Best Practice:** Provide access to quality food, fresh water, and medical care. Regular health checks and the careful observation of pigeon behavior are essential for maintaining their well-being.

Sustainability Practices

Pigeon racing, like any sport or hobby, has an environmental footprint. From the construction of lofts to the logistics of racing, several aspects of pigeon racing operations can be optimized to reduce their environmental impact.

Eco-Friendly Loft Construction

Building sustainable, energy-efficient lofts should be a priority for any pigeon racing enthusiast. Use of renewable materials, energy-efficient lighting, and insulation can reduce the loft's carbon footprint.

- **Best Practice:** Opt for natural materials such as bamboo, reclaimed wood, or recycled materials when constructing or renovating pigeon lofts. Additionally, incorporating ventilation and insulation techniques can reduce the need for excessive heating or cooling, saving energy.

Reducing Waste and Pollution

Managing waste, particularly pigeon droppings, is a crucial aspect of sustainability. Excessive waste can contribute to pollution and poor health for both the pigeons and the surrounding environment.

- **Best Practice:** Implement a waste management system that composts or safely disposes of pigeon droppings. This not only minimizes the environmental impact but can also turn waste into a valuable resource for gardening or farming. Similarly, minimize the use of chemicals and pesticides, opting for natural alternatives when possible.

Minimizing Transportation Footprint

Transportation is another significant factor in the environmental impact of pigeon racing, particularly when traveling long distances for races. Minimizing the carbon footprint of transport can be achieved through smarter logistics and carpooling with other racers.

- **Best Practice:** If traveling for races, consider using efficient vehicles with lower emissions or collaborate with other fanciers to reduce the number of trips required. Organizing group transport can also help reduce costs and minimize the environmental impact.

Regulatory Compliance

Pigeon racing is a regulated sport, with both local and international rules in place to ensure the safety and integrity of the sport, as well as the protection of the birds. Adhering to these regulations is essential for maintaining a sustainable and ethically sound operation.

Local Regulations

Each country or region may have its own set of regulations regarding the treatment of racing pigeons, breeding standards, and transport rules. These can cover everything from pigeon health requirements to specific distances for races or even breeding licenses. Fanciers must familiarize themselves with these rules to ensure they comply and avoid legal issues.

- **Best Practice:** Stay up-to-date with local laws regarding animal welfare, pigeon transport, and other regulations. Participating in pigeon racing clubs or organizations can provide valuable resources for understanding and complying with local rules.

International Regulations and Standards

International pigeon racing events often involve participants from different countries. As such, global standards for the treatment and transport of pigeons are also in place. These international regulations are crucial for ensuring fairness, safety, and the health of pigeons in a competitive environment.

- **Best Practice:** Familiarize yourself with international racing organizations like the *International Federation of Racing Pigeons* (IFRP), which sets standards for global events. Understand and adhere to international health and transport protocols when competing in international races.

Ethical Breeding and International Collaboration

In addition to health and transport regulations, international collaborations focus on ethical breeding practices. Many countries have set guidelines to ensure that breeders follow humane practices, particularly regarding genetics and genetic diversity, to avoid inbreeding and health complications in the birds.

- **Best Practice:** Collaborate with reputable international breeders who prioritize genetic diversity and the health of their pigeons. Ensure that all breeding practices meet ethical standards, as outlined by global racing associations.

Ethics and sustainability are crucial aspects of pigeon racing that must be taken into account by all participants, from hobbyists to professionals. By maintaining high ethical standards in breeding, racing, and general pigeon welfare, participants not only ensure the longevity and health of their birds but also protect the integrity of the sport. Sustainability practices, such as eco-friendly loft construction, waste management, and smarter transportation logistics, help minimize the environmental footprint of pigeon racing. Finally, adhering to both local and international regulations ensures that the sport remains fair, humane, and legally sound. By integrating these practices into their operations, pigeon racers contribute to a more ethical, sustainable, and respected future for the sport.

Innovations in Technology

Technological advancements are transforming pigeon racing, introducing tools that enhance accuracy, training, and breeding strategies. From electronic timing systems and drones to the integration of artificial intelligence, these innovations are elevating the sport, providing racers with invaluable data and methods to refine their practices.

Advanced Timing Systems

Accurate timing is a cornerstone of pigeon racing. In recent years, electronic timing systems have revolutionized how results are recorded, ensuring unparalleled precision while simplifying processes.

The Evolution of Timing Systems

Traditional timing involved manually recording a pigeon's return to the loft, which was not only time-consuming but also prone to human error. Modern electronic timing systems utilize RFID (Radio Frequency Identification) bands attached to the pigeons' legs. These bands interact with sensors at the loft to record arrival times with precision down to milliseconds.

- **Benefits:**
    - Eliminates manual errors.
    - Automates the data collection process.
    - Provides real-time updates for racers and organizers.

GPS Integration

Many timing systems now incorporate GPS technology, enabling real-time tracking of pigeons during races. GPS devices record flight paths, speeds, and distances, giving trainers and racers a comprehensive overview of the bird's performance.

- **Applications:**
    - Identifying efficient flight paths.
    - Monitoring birds' progress in long-distance races.
    - Gaining insights into environmental factors affecting performance.

Impact on Race Accuracy

The integration of electronic and GPS timing systems ensures consistent and unbiased race results, fostering fairness in competition. Furthermore, the data collected helps racers fine-tune their training programs to achieve optimal results.

Drones for Training Observation

Drone technology is providing pigeon trainers with a bird's-eye view of their flocks during training flights. These unmanned aerial vehicles (UAVs) offer an innovative way to monitor pigeons in real-time, revealing patterns and behaviors that were previously difficult to observe.

Enhancing Training with Drones

Drones equipped with cameras and sensors can track pigeons during flight, capturing data on their speed, altitude, and flight paths. This information allows trainers to assess individual and group performance.

- **Advantages:**
    - Detects deviations from the desired flight path.
    - Monitors how pigeons respond to environmental challenges.
    - Identifies signs of fatigue or distress early.

Safety Benefits

Drones are also valuable for ensuring pigeons' safety. Trainers can use drones to locate birds that have strayed from the group or assess terrain for potential hazards. Some advanced drones feature thermal imaging, allowing for tracking in low-light or adverse weather conditions.

- **Best Practices:**
  - Use drones to observe long-distance training flights.
  - Analyze footage to refine strategies for improving endurance and resilience.

AI in Breeding and Performance Prediction

Artificial intelligence (AI) is emerging as a game-changer in pigeon racing, offering new ways to optimize breeding programs and predict performance based on data rather than intuition.

AI in Breeding Programs

AI tools can analyze genetic data from multiple generations of pigeons, identifying traits associated with speed, endurance, and homing ability. By using this information, breeders can make more informed decisions about pairing pigeons to produce offspring with desirable characteristics.

- **Applications:**
  - Predicting the likelihood of high-performing offspring.
  - Balancing genetic diversity with performance goals.

o   Reducing the time required to achieve breeding objectives.

Performance Prediction

AI systems analyze data from races, such as speed, distance, and weather conditions, to forecast a pigeon's potential in specific types of races. These predictions allow racers to tailor training regimens and select optimal race entries.

- **Key Benefits:**

  o   Increases the accuracy of pigeon assessments.

  o   Reduces reliance on subjective evaluations.

  o   Guides long-term planning for races and training.

AI in Breeding Processes for Pigeons

Artificial Intelligence (AI) is transforming traditional pigeon breeding practices, offering precision and efficiency in creating superior racing pigeons. By analyzing extensive datasets, AI can help breeders make data-driven decisions to produce pigeons with desirable traits while maintaining genetic diversity and reducing the time it takes to achieve optimal outcomes.

How AI Revolutionizes Breeding

AI uses advanced algorithms to analyze genetic, performance, and environmental data. By identifying patterns and correlations, it provides insights into which pairs are likely to produce offspring with superior racing abilities. Here's how it works:

1. **Data Collection**:

   o Genetic information: Pedigree records, DNA sequencing, and heritable traits like endurance, speed, and homing instincts.

   o Performance metrics: Historical race results, speed, flight patterns, and recovery times.

   o Environmental factors: Breeding conditions, diet, and loft environments.

2. **Data Analysis**:
   AI algorithms process this data to identify patterns, such as which genetic combinations are linked to specific traits. For instance, a combination of genes may indicate stronger navigation abilities or resistance to fatigue.

3. **Trait Prediction**:
   AI predicts the likelihood of offspring inheriting key traits from their parents. This includes physical attributes like wing structure and muscle mass, as well as behavioral traits like homing instinct and resilience under pressure.

4. **Optimizing Pairings**:

   o **Trait Maximization**: Breeders can use AI to select pairs with complementary traits, ensuring offspring inherit a balance of speed, endurance, and intelligence.

- o **Genetic Diversity**: AI avoids inbreeding by identifying pairs that maintain healthy genetic variation, which is essential for long-term breeding success.

The Role of Machine Learning in Breeding

Machine learning, a subset of AI, uses historical data to improve its predictions over time. As breeders input more information about their pigeons, such as the results of pairings and race performances, the system refines its algorithms for even greater accuracy.

- **Iterative Learning**: Each new breeding cycle contributes to the AI's database, improving its ability to recommend pairings that yield high-performing pigeons.

- **Customized Insights**: AI can tailor recommendations based on a breeder's specific goals, whether for short-distance speed races or long-distance endurance events.

Practical Applications of AI in Breeding

1. **Genetic Compatibility Scoring**:
   AI assigns compatibility scores to potential breeding pairs based on their genetic profiles. This helps breeders prioritize pairings with the highest likelihood of producing exceptional offspring.

2. **Simulation of Outcomes**:

- o   AI simulates potential outcomes of different pairings, showing breeders the probability of specific traits in the offspring.

- o   Breeders can visualize scenarios before committing to a breeding plan.

3. **Targeted Trait Enhancement**:
    For breeders aiming to improve specific traits, such as long-distance navigation or rapid recovery, AI identifies pigeons with a history of excelling in those areas. Pairings can then be designed to enhance these traits across generations.

AI-Driven Genetic Testing

With the integration of genetic testing, AI can work more effectively by incorporating data from DNA sequencing. Genetic testing reveals markers linked to traits like immune system strength, muscle development, and navigation ability. AI uses this data to refine its predictions further.

- **Identifying Hidden Potential**: Genetic testing uncovers traits not visible in the physical appearance or race history of a pigeon. AI leverages this information to recommend non-obvious pairings that might yield extraordinary results.

- **Disease Resistance**: AI can identify pigeons with genetic markers for robust immune systems, ensuring healthier offspring with fewer vulnerabilities.

Ethical Considerations in AI Breeding

While AI offers unparalleled precision, it also raises ethical questions about the role of technology in breeding. Breeders must strike a balance between leveraging AI and maintaining humane practices:

- **Animal Welfare**: Avoid overbreeding or culling pigeons based solely on AI predictions.

- **Transparency**: Clearly communicate how AI is used in breeding to ensure fair competition in races.

Future of AI in Pigeon Breeding

As technology advances, the role of AI in pigeon breeding will continue to expand. Potential developments include:

- **Real-Time Monitoring**: Combining AI with wearable devices for pigeons to track health and performance in real-time, providing immediate feedback for breeding decisions.

- **Integration with CRISPR**: AI-guided gene editing could one day enable targeted improvements in racing traits while adhering to ethical standards.

Step-by-Step Guide: Applying AI to Racing Pigeons

Artificial Intelligence (AI) has become a revolutionary tool in pigeon racing, offering precision and insights that were previously unattainable. Below is a comprehensive guide on how to implement AI in your racing pigeon operations:

Racing Pigeons Mastery Unleashed

1. Define Objectives for AI Implementation

Before starting, clarify the goals you want to achieve using AI. Common objectives include:

- Enhancing breeding programs for performance traits.

- Analyzing race data for better strategy development.

- Monitoring pigeon health and fitness.

2. Gather Data

AI systems rely on robust data sets. Begin by collecting and organizing relevant data about your pigeons.

Types of Data to Collect:

- **Pedigree Information**: Lineage and breeding history.

- **Physical Attributes**: Wing span, weight, and muscle density.

- **Race Data**: Flight speeds, distances, times, and environmental conditions.

- **Health Records**: Vaccination schedules, illnesses, and recovery times.

- **Behavioral Data**: Training habits, feeding times, and loft activities.

Tools for Data Collection:

- GPS trackers for race performance.

- Smart loft systems for real-time monitoring.

- Health tracking apps or IoT devices for vitals.

3. Choose an AI Platform

Select a platform or software that specializes in AI applications for animal breeding or sports analytics.

Recommended Tools:

- **AI Breeding Platforms**: Programs like ZooEasy or Aviagen for analyzing genetic data.

- **Race Data Analysis Tools**: Custom AI algorithms or platforms like Tableau for data visualization.

- **Health Monitoring Systems**: AI-based tools for predicting diseases or tracking fitness trends.

4. Set Up Data Infrastructure

Ensure you have a system to store, process, and analyze the data.

Steps:

1. **Create a Database**: Use software like Microsoft Excel, Google Sheets, or advanced databases like MySQL for data storage.

2. **Integrate Data Collection Devices**: Connect GPS trackers, cameras, and health monitors to your central database.

3. **Cloud Storage**: Opt for cloud-based solutions like Google Drive or AWS for scalability and remote access.

5. Train the AI Model

Develop or customize an AI model to analyze your pigeon data and provide actionable insights.

Training Process:

1. **Data Cleaning**: Remove inconsistencies or irrelevant information to ensure accuracy.

2. **Input Historical Data**: Use past race and breeding records to train the AI model.

3. **Set Parameters**: Define the key traits or outcomes you want the AI to predict, such as speed, endurance, or health risks.

4. **Run Simulations**: Test the model with various scenarios to refine its predictions.

Tools for Model Development:

- **Google TensorFlow**: For building custom AI models.

- **Pre-built AI Solutions**: Platforms like IBM Watson or Azure AI for accessible analytics.

6. Apply AI to Breeding

Utilize AI insights to refine your breeding programs.

Steps:

1. **Analyze Genetic Data**: Use AI to identify pigeons with desirable traits, such as stamina or homing ability.

2. **Pair Selection**: AI suggests optimal breeding pairs based on genetic compatibility and performance history.

3. **Monitor Outcomes**: Track the success of breeding decisions by analyzing offspring performance over time.

7. Use AI for Race Strategy

Improve your racing strategy using AI-driven insights.

Steps:

1. **Analyze Historical Races**:

   o   Study weather patterns, race distances, and pigeon performance to identify trends.

2. **Predict Performance**:

   o   Use AI to simulate how pigeons might perform under specific conditions.

3. **Optimize Training**:

    o   Adjust training routines based on performance analytics provided by AI.

8. Monitor Health with AI

Leverage AI tools to ensure pigeons remain in peak condition.

Steps:

1. **Track Vital Signs**: Use IoT devices or health trackers to monitor heart rate, weight, and respiratory health.

2. **Detect Early Warnings**: AI algorithms can flag abnormal patterns, such as sudden weight loss or irregular flight data, indicating potential health issues.

3. **Plan Preventative Care**: Use AI insights to schedule vaccinations, deworming, or other health measures proactively.

9. Evaluate and Refine the System

Regularly assess the effectiveness of your AI implementation.

Steps:

1. **Review Predictions**: Compare AI forecasts with actual results to gauge accuracy.

2. **Incorporate Feedback**: Adjust algorithms or data inputs based on observed discrepancies.

3. **Upgrade Technology**: Stay updated with the latest AI tools and techniques to maintain competitive advantages.

10. Train Yourself and Your Team

AI tools are only as effective as the people using them.

Steps:

1. **Learn the Basics**: Understand AI principles and how they apply to pigeon racing.

2. **Attend Workshops**: Enroll in AI or data science courses tailored for animal breeding or sports analytics.

3. **Collaborate with Experts**: Partner with data scientists or AI developers to optimize your system.

By following this guide, you can integrate AI into your pigeon racing operations, enhancing breeding programs, optimizing race strategies, and ensuring superior health management. With consistent use and refinement, AI can significantly elevate your pigeons' performance and your success as a racer.

AI breeding processes provide a significant leap forward in the quest to develop the ultimate racing pigeon. By analyzing vast amounts of data and making precise predictions, AI enables breeders to refine their methods, reduce trial-and-error cycles, and achieve remarkable results. When combined with traditional expertise and ethical practices, AI can elevate pigeon racing to unprecedented heights.

The incorporation of advanced timing systems, drones, and AI into pigeon racing marks a new era for the sport. These technologies offer unprecedented insights into training, breeding, and performance, allowing enthusiasts to make data-driven decisions that enhance results. By adopting these innovations, pigeon racers can stay competitive while ensuring the welfare and success of their birds.

Advanced Health and Recovery Practices

Maintaining optimal health and ensuring swift recovery are cornerstones of successful pigeon racing. With advances in science and technology, pigeon enthusiasts now have access to innovative techniques and tools that promote longevity, enhance performance, and expedite recovery. This chapter delves into these advanced health and recovery practices, ensuring your pigeons remain at the peak of their potential.

Post-Race Recovery Science

Racing is an intense physical and mental challenge for pigeons, requiring meticulous recovery protocols to restore their energy and readiness for subsequent competitions.

1. **Specialized Diets**:

     o **Replenishing Glycogen Stores**: Pigeons lose significant energy during races, primarily glycogen stored in their muscles and liver. High-carbohydrate grains like corn and millet can help restore these levels effectively.

- o **Protein for Muscle Repair**: Incorporating protein-rich seeds such as peas and lentils aids in repairing muscle tissues stressed during flight.

- o **Micronutrient Support**: Adding vitamins and minerals like vitamin E, magnesium, and potassium to their diet supports recovery by reducing oxidative stress and replenishing electrolytes.

2. **Hydration Protocols**:

- o **Electrolyte Solutions**: Specialized hydration mixtures containing sodium, potassium, and chloride combat dehydration and help restore fluid balance after a race.

- o **Hydration Timing**: Providing water infused with electrolytes within 30 minutes of a pigeon's return maximizes absorption and recovery efficiency.

3. **Rest and Recovery**:

- o **Scheduled Rest Days**: Allowing pigeons at least 48–72 hours of rest post-race is crucial for muscle recovery and mental rejuvenation.

- o **Quiet Recovery Environment**: Ensuring a stress-free, comfortable loft environment minimizes additional strain during recovery.

Preventative Medicine and Genetic Screening

Preventing diseases before they manifest is a proactive approach that enhances a pigeon's overall health and longevity. Combining advanced diagnostic techniques with routine care ensures your pigeons remain in top form.

1. **Early Diagnostics**:

   o **Routine Health Checks**: Regular screenings, including fecal tests and blood work, can detect early signs of infections or deficiencies.

   o **Thermal Imaging**: Modern tools like thermal cameras identify areas of inflammation or potential injury, even before symptoms appear.

2. **Genetic Screening**:

   o **Identifying Hereditary Conditions**: Genetic testing helps pinpoint pigeons predisposed to certain diseases, allowing breeders to make informed breeding decisions.

   o **Performance Traits Analysis**: Screening for genes associated with endurance, speed, or immunity helps identify potential champions early in their development.

3. **Vaccination Programs**:

   o Establish a comprehensive vaccination schedule targeting common pigeon diseases like paramyxovirus and salmonellosis to ensure flock immunity.

4. **Dietary Supplements**:

   o Preventative supplements, such as probiotics
   and omega-3 fatty acids, boost gut health
   and reduce inflammation, preventing long-
   term issues.

Therapeutic Practices

In addition to traditional treatments, innovative therapeutic
techniques are being explored to enhance recovery and
manage injuries effectively.

1. **Light Therapy**:

   o **Red and Infrared Light**: This therapy
   promotes tissue repair by increasing blood
   flow and reducing inflammation. It is
   particularly effective for treating muscle
   strain and minor injuries.

   o **Application**: Lightweight LED devices can
   be used directly on injured areas or
   incorporated into loft design for general
   wellness.

2. **Acupuncture**:

   o **Ancient Meets Modern**: Acupuncture,
   adapted for use in birds, can alleviate pain,
   improve circulation, and reduce stress.

   o **Applications**: Experienced veterinarians can
   use this therapy to treat musculoskeletal

injuries or optimize recovery after rigorous training sessions.

3. **Hydrotherapy**:

   o **Controlled Water Exercises**: Hydrotherapy allows pigeons to exercise without stressing their joints and muscles, facilitating recovery and rehabilitation.

4. **Massage Therapy**:

   o **Improving Circulation**: Gentle massage techniques help relax tight muscles, reduce swelling, and improve overall circulation.

Creating a Comprehensive Recovery Plan

1. **Individualized Care**:
   Tailor recovery plans to each pigeon's needs, considering factors like age, race distance, and health history.

2. **Tracking Progress**:
   Use tools such as digital scales to monitor weight fluctuations, and GPS trackers to evaluate post-recovery flight performance.

3. **Incorporating Technology**:

   o Wearable health monitors provide real-time insights into a pigeon's vitals, including heart rate and respiratory efficiency, during recovery.

- o Smartphone apps can help track recovery milestones and flag potential health concerns.

Advanced health and recovery practices combine science, technology, and tradition to provide racing pigeons with the best care possible. By focusing on post-race recovery, preventative medicine, and therapeutic treatments, breeders and racers can ensure their pigeons achieve peak performance and sustain long, healthy lives.

Exploring Pigeon Racing as a Business

Pigeon racing, beyond being a passion and sport, has the potential to be a lucrative business. With careful planning, professional practices, and strategic marketing, enthusiasts can transform their expertise into a thriving enterprise. This chapter outlines the key components for establishing and scaling a business in pigeon racing, from breeding operations to marketing strategies and branding.

Professional Breeding Operations

Setting up a large-scale breeding program requires meticulous planning, investment in quality stock, and the application of advanced techniques.

1. Designing the Breeding Facility

- **Infrastructure:** Construct spacious, climate-controlled lofts equipped with sections for breeding pairs, rearing young birds, and isolation for health monitoring.

- **Technology Integration:** Implement automated systems for feeding, watering, and monitoring environmental conditions.

- **Biosecurity Measures:** Ensure strict hygiene protocols to prevent disease spread, including footbaths, air filtration systems, and regular sanitation.

2. Selecting and Maintaining Quality Stock

- **Sourcing Stock:** Invest in high-performance pigeons with proven pedigrees from reputable breeders.

- **Pair Selection:** Use data-driven techniques or AI tools to select optimal breeding pairs based on desirable traits like speed, endurance, and homing instincts.

- **Health Management:** Conduct regular health checks and provide vaccinations, deworming, and nutritional supplements to maintain stock quality.

3. Scaling the Operation

- **Expansion:** Gradually increase the number of breeding pairs as demand grows, ensuring that quality standards are maintained.

- **Staffing:** Hire experienced handlers, trainers, and veterinarians to assist in managing large-scale operations.

- **Sustainability Practices:** Adopt environmentally friendly practices, such as waste recycling and energy-efficient systems, to enhance long-term viability.

Marketing High-Value Pigeons

Creating demand for your pigeons requires strategic marketing, focusing on their unique qualities and achievements.

1. Showcasing Pedigrees and Achievements

- **Performance Records:** Highlight race wins, exceptional speed, or consistency in flight performance.

- **Pedigree Charts:** Display detailed lineage information, emphasizing connections to renowned bloodlines.

- **Health Certification:** Provide documentation of health screenings and vaccinations to reassure buyers of the pigeons' condition.

2. Utilizing Digital Platforms

- **Website Development:** Create a professional website showcasing available pigeons, success stories, and breeding programs.

- **Social Media:** Share updates, race results, and behind-the-scenes content on platforms like Facebook, Instagram, and YouTube to engage with the community.

- **Online Auctions:** Use platforms like PIPA or specialized pigeon racing marketplaces to reach global buyers.

3. Networking and Events

- **Pigeon Shows and Expos:** Attend local and international exhibitions to showcase your birds and connect with potential buyers.

- **Collaborations:** Partner with other breeders or racing teams to enhance visibility and credibility.

- **Community Engagement:** Host workshops, webinars, or live training sessions to establish yourself as an authority in the field.

Building a Brand in Pigeon Racing

Developing a strong reputation is key to standing out in the competitive world of pigeon racing.

1. Defining Your Unique Value Proposition

- **Specialization:** Identify what sets your pigeons apart, such as unique bloodlines, advanced training methods, or success in specific race types.

- **Commitment to Quality:** Emphasize ethical practices, excellent care, and proven results as the foundation of your brand.

2. Creating a Recognizable Identity

- **Logo and Branding:** Develop a professional logo and consistent branding for your loft, including loft names and promotional materials.

- **Storytelling:** Share your journey, successes, and challenges to create an emotional connection with your audience.

- **Merchandising:** Offer branded items such as T-shirts, caps, and calendars to spread awareness and foster loyalty.

3. Building Trust and Authority

- **Customer Testimonials:** Collect and share feedback from satisfied buyers or collaborators.

- **Educational Content:** Publish books, articles, or videos about pigeon care, breeding, and racing to demonstrate expertise.

- **Race Participation:** Actively compete in high-profile races to prove the quality of your pigeons and enhance credibility.

Exploring pigeon racing as a business requires dedication, innovation, and a focus on quality. By implementing professional breeding practices, leveraging effective marketing strategies, and building a strong brand, you can transform your passion for pigeons into a successful enterprise. Whether your goal is to establish a global reputation or simply earn supplemental income, a structured approach will ensure long-term success.

Legal and Financial Aspects of Pigeon Racing

As pigeon racing continues to grow globally, enthusiasts and professionals must be aware of the legal and financial dimensions of the sport. This chapter delves into navigating local and international regulations, securing appropriate insurance for high-value pigeons, and identifying ways to monetize success in competitive pigeon racing.

Navigating Legalities

Pigeon racing involves various laws and regulations, depending on the country and region where the activity is conducted. Understanding these legalities is crucial to avoid penalties and ensure smooth operations.

1. **Local   Regulations**
   Many jurisdictions have specific rules governing the ownership, housing, and training of pigeons. This may include permits for keeping lofts, restrictions on the number of birds, and guidelines on sanitation and

waste management. Familiarize yourself with these rules by consulting local animal control agencies or racing organizations.

2. **International   Laws**
    For racers involved in global competitions or the trade of pigeons across borders, understanding international laws is vital. Key considerations include:

    o   Compliance with **CITES (Convention on International Trade in Endangered Species)** for any bird species that may fall under protected categories.

    o   Adhering to quarantine and health certification requirements for exporting or importing pigeons.

    o   Customs regulations, including proper documentation for shipment and transport.

3. **Racing   Guidelines**
    Membership in pigeon racing associations often requires adherence to specific rules. These can include guidelines on the timing systems used, race conduct, and treatment of pigeons. Study the policies of organizations such as the International Federation of American Homing Pigeon Fanciers (IF) or other regional bodies.

Insurance for High-Value Pigeons

Champion racing pigeons can be incredibly valuable, with some fetching thousands or even millions of dollars. Protecting these assets with insurance is a smart decision for any professional breeder or racer.

1. **Types of Coverage**
   Insurance for pigeons typically includes:

   - **Mortality Insurance**: Covers the value of the bird in the event of death due to illness, injury, or accident.

   - **Theft Insurance**: Protects against loss due to theft, especially for lofts housing valuable birds.

   - **Transport Insurance**: Ensures coverage during travel to competitions or sales events.

2. **Choosing a Provider**
   Specialist insurance providers often cater to niche markets like pigeon racing. When selecting a provider:

   - Ensure they have experience in animal insurance.

   - Compare policy terms, premiums, and claim processes.

   - Verify whether the policy covers international transport and competition.

3. **Valuation and Documentation**
   Insuring high-value pigeons requires proper documentation, including:

- o   Pedigree records.

- o   Race performance history.

- o   Professional valuation reports.

Monetizing Success

Pigeon racing offers numerous opportunities to generate income. Leveraging success through sponsorships, partnerships, and prize money can turn passion into profit.

1. **Sponsorships   and   Partnerships**
   Many companies are interested in partnering with successful racers to promote their products. Opportunities include:

   - o   Loft branding and naming rights.

   - o   Endorsement deals for pigeon supplies such as feed, supplements, or technology.

   - o   Collaboration with media outlets to showcase races or breeding programs.

2. **Prize   Money**
   Competitive pigeon racing often features significant cash rewards, particularly in large-scale international events. Examples include the Million Dollar Pigeon Race and regional grand prix events. To maximize earnings:

   - o   Focus on breeding and training high-caliber pigeons.

   - o   Participate in multiple competitions to diversify opportunities.

3. **Selling   High-Value   Pigeons**
Breeding and selling pigeons with exceptional pedigrees can be highly lucrative. Key tips include:

   o Highlighting the bird's lineage and race achievements in advertisements.

   o Building a network of international buyers.

   o Utilizing online platforms and auctions to reach a global audience.

4. **Educational   and   Consulting   Services**
Experienced breeders and racers can monetize their expertise by offering:

   o Training workshops and seminars.

   o Paid consultations for loft design, breeding, or race preparation.

   o Publishing books or creating digital courses on pigeon racing.

Understanding and addressing the legal and financial aspects of pigeon racing is essential for long-term success. By navigating the regulations, securing adequate insurance, and capitalizing on monetization opportunities, pigeon racers can protect their investments and maximize the profitability of their endeavors. These steps not only ensure compliance and security but also lay the foundation for a sustainable and thriving career in pigeon racing.

The Future of Pigeon Racing

Pigeon racing, steeped in history and tradition, is undergoing transformative changes driven by technological advancements, evolving trends, and increasing focus on sustainability. This chapter explores the future of the sport, delving into innovations reshaping its organization, the role of technology, and the steps needed to address environmental concerns.

Emerging Trends in the Sport

The world of pigeon racing is evolving, with modern innovations changing how races are organized, monitored, and judged. These trends not only enhance the sport's fairness but also broaden its appeal.

1. **Digital Race Management**
   Many pigeon racing clubs are adopting digital platforms to streamline race administration. These platforms handle race registrations, scheduling, and results reporting with precision and efficiency, eliminating paperwork and reducing human errors.

2. **Globalization of Competitions**
   The increased connectivity among pigeon enthusiasts worldwide has led to more international races. Global events such as the Million Dollar Pigeon Race showcase the sport's ability to transcend borders, bringing together participants from diverse cultures and regions.

3. **Diversity in Participation**
   Pigeon racing is no longer limited to traditional participants. There is a noticeable rise in younger

enthusiasts and individuals from urban areas who see the sport as both a hobby and an investment opportunity. This shift is attributed to better accessibility through online communities and platforms.

4. **Focus on Welfare and Ethics**
   There is growing awareness and advocacy for ethical treatment of pigeons in racing. Regulatory bodies are implementing stricter guidelines to ensure the welfare of birds during training, racing, and breeding, encouraging transparency and accountability.

The Role of Technology in Pigeon Racing's Evolution

Technology has revolutionized pigeon racing, enhancing the precision, efficiency, and enjoyment of the sport. The integration of advanced tools and systems is setting the stage for a new era.

1. **Electronic Timing Systems**
   The advent of electronic timing systems has transformed race accuracy. These systems automatically record a pigeon's arrival, eliminating manual errors and providing real-time updates for participants and spectators.

2. **GPS Tracking**
   GPS devices attached to pigeons enable detailed tracking of flight paths, speeds, and distances. This data offers insights into a bird's performance, helping trainers refine their strategies and identify areas for improvement.

3. **Artificial Intelligence (AI)**
   AI is increasingly being used to analyze data from training sessions and races. It can predict a pigeon's potential performance, optimize breeding selections, and even design personalized training programs based on individual strengths and weaknesses.

4. **Drones for Training and Observation**
   Drones are emerging as a tool for monitoring pigeons during training flights. They provide a bird's-eye view of the flock, helping trainers identify patterns, track progress, and ensure safety during long-distance exercises.

5. **Virtual Communities and Platforms**
   Online forums, social media groups, and specialized apps allow enthusiasts to connect, exchange ideas, and even participate in virtual races. These platforms foster a sense of community and promote knowledge-sharing among pigeon racers worldwide.

Pigeon Racing and Environmental Concerns

As global attention shifts toward sustainability, pigeon racing must adapt to address environmental challenges. Balancing tradition with modern eco-friendly practices will be crucial for the sport's long-term viability.

1. **Minimizing Carbon Footprint**
   The transportation of pigeons to race locations contributes to carbon emissions. To reduce this impact, organizers are exploring:

- o **Regionalized Races**: Encouraging local competitions to minimize long-distance travel.

- o **Green Logistics**: Using energy-efficient vehicles or carbon-offset programs for transportation.

2. **Eco-Friendly Loft Design**
Modern lofts are being designed with sustainability in mind. Features such as solar panels, rainwater harvesting systems, and natural ventilation not only reduce environmental impact but also create healthier habitats for the pigeons.

3. **Responsible Breeding Practices**
Overbreeding can strain resources and lead to surplus birds that may not find suitable homes. Responsible breeding focuses on quality over quantity, ensuring that each bird is well-cared-for and has a meaningful role in the flock.

4. **Promoting Awareness**
Clubs and associations are increasingly promoting environmental education within the community. By highlighting the importance of sustainable practices, they inspire participants to make eco-conscious choices.

The future of pigeon racing is an exciting blend of tradition and innovation. Emerging trends and advancements in technology are reshaping the sport, making it more inclusive, efficient, and enjoyable. At the same time, addressing environmental concerns ensures its sustainability for future generations. By embracing change and prioritizing ethical and eco-friendly practices, pigeon racing can continue to thrive as a respected and cherished activity worldwide.

CHAPTER THIRTY-FIVE

ADDITIONAL RESOURCES

To make this guide indispensable to both beginners and experts, this chapter provides essential additional resources that can elevate your understanding of pigeon racing. By offering exclusive insights from world champions, a global directory of resources, and advanced templates for record-keeping, we aim to equip you with tools and knowledge that go beyond basic pigeon care and training. Whether you are striving for competitive success or simply enhancing your involvement in the sport, these resources are designed to support you on every step of your journey.

Interviews with World Champions

Success in pigeon racing is often a result of years of dedication, research, and refined strategies. In this section, we share exclusive insights from some of the most accomplished pigeon racers around the world. These champions have reached the pinnacle of the sport, overcome countless challenges and perfecting their techniques. By exploring their experiences, strategies, and philosophies, you can gain valuable perspectives that could influence your own racing approach.

1. **Training   Strategies**

   World champions emphasize the importance of individualized training plans. They stress the necessity of understanding each bird's unique strengths and weaknesses. By tailoring training exercises to suit each bird, they maximize performance during competition. Many champions incorporate long-distance flights gradually, starting with shorter training sessions and gradually increasing the distance as the birds build endurance and confidence.

2. **Managing Health and Wellness**
Maintaining the health of racing pigeons is critical to success, and the champions interviewed focus heavily on preventative care. Regular veterinary check-ups, specialized diets, and proper hydration protocols are essential in keeping pigeons in peak condition. Most racers also advocate for a holistic approach to pigeon health, which includes minimizing stress and fostering a comfortable environment within the loft.

3. **Race Day Preparation**
The final days leading up to a race are crucial. Top-tier racers are meticulous in their preparation, ensuring that the pigeons are well-rested, properly fed, and free from distractions. They emphasize the importance of a quiet, undisturbed environment in the days leading to the race, as pigeons need to be calm and focused for the journey ahead.

4. **Overcoming Challenges**
Every racer faces setbacks, from bad weather conditions to unforeseen health issues in their birds. Champions often attribute their success to their ability to adapt and persist in the face of adversity. For them, resilience is a key trait that helps them overcome challenges, learn from failures, and continually improve their methods.

Global Resource Directory

To make your involvement in pigeon racing even more fruitful, we have compiled a comprehensive directory of international resources. This directory connects you with top breeders, racing clubs, and suppliers worldwide, allowing you to tap into a vast network of expertise and high-quality products that can enhance your racing experience.

1. **Pigeon   Racing   Clubs**
   Across the globe, pigeon racing clubs play a pivotal role in organizing races, offering training resources, and fostering a sense of community. Each club has its unique focus, with some specializing in local races and others facilitating international competitions. The directory includes contact details, websites, and membership information for clubs in North America, Europe, Asia, and beyond.

2. **Breeders   and   Suppliers**
   Whether you're looking for high-performance racing pigeons or specialized loft equipment, the directory provides a list of reputable breeders and suppliers. You can find breeders who focus on specific pigeon breeds, such as middle-distance or long-distance racers, and suppliers offering everything from feed to advanced timing systems.

3. **Veterinary Services and Health Professionals**
   Maintaining the health of your pigeons is critical, and this section of the directory connects you with specialized veterinary services that focus on pigeon care. From routine health checks to emergency care, these professionals understand the unique needs of racing pigeons and offer tailored services to help keep your birds in peak condition.

4. **Training and Consulting Experts**
   For those looking to take their pigeon racing skills to the next level, the directory also includes a list of expert trainers and consultants who offer personalized coaching. These professionals bring years of experience and advanced strategies to help you refine your techniques and optimize your birds' performance.

Templates for Record-Keeping

Successful pigeon racing requires meticulous attention to detail, and keeping accurate records is essential. This section provides advanced logs and templates for tracking essential data, including training routines, health checks, and race results. Proper record-keeping allows you to monitor your pigeons' progress, identify patterns, and make data-driven decisions that enhance your racing success.

1. **Training Logs**
   Tracking each bird's training progress is vital for identifying strengths, weaknesses, and areas that need improvement. The training log templates include sections for recording flight distances, times, weather conditions, and any specific notes related to the bird's performance or behavior. Regularly updating these logs will help you tailor your training plans and track your pigeons' improvements over time.

2. **Health and Wellness Records**
   Keeping a record of health check-ups, vaccinations, dietary changes, and other relevant medical information is essential for maintaining your birds' well-being. These templates allow you to document each pigeon's health history, providing a

comprehensive overview that will be helpful for making informed decisions about care and treatment.

3. **Race Data Tracking**
   To measure your pigeons' competitive performance, detailed race data logs are a must. These templates allow you to record race results, including flight times, rankings, and any external factors such as weather conditions that may have influenced the outcome. Over time, you will be able to analyze this data to detect trends, gauge performance, and identify areas for improvement in future races.

4. **Breeding Logs**
   For breeders, detailed records of breeding pairs, offspring, and their subsequent performance in races can be invaluable. The breeding log templates allow you to track genetic lines, monitor the performance of individual birds, and ensure that breeding decisions are made based on both pedigree and performance data.

This chapter serves as a powerful resource for pigeon racing enthusiasts, providing valuable insights from world champions, a comprehensive directory of global resources, and practical tools to keep track of essential data. Whether you're just beginning your racing journey or are looking to optimize your advanced strategies, these resources are designed to empower you with the knowledge and support you need to succeed in the world of pigeon racing.

FAQ
General Questions About Pigeon Racing

1. **What is pigeon racing, and how does it work?**
Pigeon racing involves releasing trained homing pigeons from a specific location and timing their return to their loft. The pigeon with the fastest time wins.

2. **How do homing pigeons find their way back?**
Homing pigeons use a combination of magnetic fields, olfactory cues, and visual landmarks to navigate back to their lofts.

3. **What is the history of pigeon racing?**
Pigeon racing dates back thousands of years, with origins in ancient Egypt and Rome, and it became a formal sport in the 19th century.

4. **Are there specific breeds of pigeons used for racing?**
Yes, racing pigeons are a specialized breed known as *Homing Pigeons*, bred for speed, endurance, and navigational abilities.

5. **How long can a racing pigeon fly in one race?**
Racing pigeons can fly up to 600 miles in a single race, depending on their training and physical condition.

6. **What are the major global pigeon racing competitions?**
Major competitions include the Million Dollar Pigeon Race, the Barcelona International, and the South African Million Dollar Race.

7. **How is a winner determined in pigeon racing?**
Winners are determined by calculating the time it takes for a pigeon to return divided by the distance covered, giving the fastest velocity.

8. **Is pigeon racing an expensive sport to start?**
It can be moderate to expensive, depending on the cost of lofts, pigeons, training, and racing equipment.

9. **What are the best locations for pigeon lofts?**
Pigeon lofts should be placed in areas with good ventilation, ample sunlight, and minimal noise or disturbance.

10. **What is the average lifespan of a racing pigeon?**
Racing pigeons live 10-15 years, but their competitive years are usually between 2 and 7 years.

Training Racing Pigeons

11. **At what age should I start training my pigeons?**
Training should start when pigeons are about 6-8 weeks old, beginning with short distances near the loft.

12. **What techniques can I use to improve my pigeons' speed?**
Consistent flight training, proper diet, and gradual distance increases help improve speed and endurance.

13. **How do I introduce my pigeons to longer-distance training?**
Start with short distances and gradually increase by 5-10 miles each week, ensuring they are comfortable at each stage.

14. **Can pigeons race in all types of weather?**
Pigeons can race in various weather conditions but may struggle with extreme heat, cold, or strong winds.

15. **What is the role of diet in a pigeon's performance?**
A balanced diet rich in carbohydrates, proteins, and essential vitamins is crucial for maintaining energy and health.

16. **How do I prevent overtraining my pigeons?**
Allow sufficient rest days, monitor fatigue signs, and adjust training intensity as needed.

17. **What is the best way to track a pigeon's progress during training?**
Use GPS tracking systems or electronic timers to monitor flight paths, speeds, and returns.

18. **Are there tools or technology to help with training?**
Yes, drones, GPS trackers, and mobile apps are available to assist in observing and analyzing training sessions.

19. **How can I ensure my pigeons stay motivated?**
Regularly change training routes and provide rewards like special feed upon their return.

20. **What are the signs that a pigeon is ready for racing?**
A healthy weight, steady training performance, and strong homing instincts indicate readiness.

Health and Care for Racing Pigeons

21. **What are the most common health issues in racing pigeons?**
Common issues include respiratory infections, coccidiosis, and paramyxovirus.

22. **How often should I take my pigeons to the vet?**
Pigeons should have annual health checks and additional visits if signs of illness appear.

23. **What vaccinations do racing pigeons need?**
Pigeons require vaccinations for paramyxovirus and, in some cases, pigeon pox.

24. **How do I ensure proper loft hygiene?**
Regular cleaning, disinfecting surfaces, and good ventilation are essential.

25. **What are the signs of stress in pigeons?**
Stress signs include reduced appetite, lethargy, and excessive feather plucking.

26. **What is the best way to treat injured pigeons?**
Isolate the injured pigeon, clean wounds, and consult a vet for severe injuries.

27. **How do I prevent diseases in a large flock?**
Practice biosecurity, ensure vaccinations, and maintain loft cleanliness.

28. **Are probiotics helpful for pigeons?**
Yes, probiotics support gut health, boost immunity, and improve digestion.

29. **How can I improve my pigeons' recovery after a race?**

Provide electrolyte-rich water, rest, and a high-protein diet for muscle repair.

30. **What are the best supplements for racing pigeons?**
Supplements like amino acids, vitamins, and minerals enhance performance and recovery.

Breeding Racing Pigeons

31. **How do I select the best pigeons for breeding?**
Choose pigeons with strong racing records, good health, and desirable traits.

32. **What is line breeding, and how does it work?**
Line breeding involves mating related pigeons to reinforce desirable traits.

33. **Should I use artificial insemination for my pigeons?**
AI allows for precise pairings and is effective for rare or high-value birds.

34. **How do I ensure genetic diversity in my flock?**
Introduce new bloodlines periodically to avoid inbreeding.

35. **At what age can pigeons start breeding?**
Pigeons can breed from 6 months old, but 1 year is ideal for maturity.

36. **How often can a pair of pigeons' breeds in a year?**
A pair can breed up to 4-5 times a year, depending on health and conditions.

37. **What should I feed breeding pigeons for optimal fertility?**

High-protein diets with added vitamins and calcium promote fertility.

38. **How do I care for baby pigeons after hatching?**
Ensure parents are feeding them, monitor growth, and maintain loft hygiene.

39. **What is epigenetics, and how does it affect breeding?**
Epigenetics studies how environmental factors influence gene expression, affecting offspring traits.

40. **Are there specific records I should keep for my breeding program?**
Yes, maintain records of lineage, performance, and health of all breeding pairs.

Pigeon Racing as a Business

41. **How can I monetize my pigeon racing skills?**
Through prize winnings, breeding programs, and selling high-value pigeons.

42. **What are the best ways to market high-value pigeons?**
Use online platforms, auctions, and networking in the pigeon racing community.

43. **How do I start a professional pigeon breeding operation?**
Invest in quality pigeons, build proper lofts, and focus on record-keeping.

44. **How can I build a strong reputation in the pigeon racing community?**
Participate in competitions, provide excellent care, and network with breeders.

45. **What are the legal requirements for selling pigeons internationally?**
Follow import/export regulations, health certifications, and quarantine rules.

46. **Should I get insurance for my pigeons?**
Yes, especially for high-value pigeons, to cover theft, injury, or loss.

47. **How do I network with global pigeon racers and breeders?**
Attend events, join forums, and participate in international competitions.

48. **What are the most effective platforms for selling racing pigeons?**
Online platforms like specialized auction sites and pigeon racing forums.

49. **How do sponsorships work in pigeon racing?**
Sponsors provide funding in exchange for brand promotion through races or pigeons.

50. **What financial records should I keep for my pigeon racing business?**
Track expenses, revenues, pigeon sales, and competition earnings.

CONCLUSION

Pigeon racing is a sport of dedication, strategy, and deep appreciation for the remarkable abilities of these extraordinary birds. Through the chapters of this book, we have delved into every facet of this fascinating world—from the foundational principles of breeding, training, and health care to the advanced strategies and technologies that are redefining the sport. Each topic has been carefully explored to provide a comprehensive guide for enthusiasts, whether they are just beginning their journey or striving to achieve mastery.

The insights shared by world champions highlight the relentless pursuit of excellence and innovation in pigeon racing. Their experiences remind us that success comes from a harmonious blend of science, intuition, and passion. By learning from their strategies, adapting their techniques, and overcoming challenges, racers can elevate their performance to new heights.

The global directory of resources emphasizes the importance of community and connection in pigeon racing. By engaging with clubs, breeders, and experts, racers can expand their knowledge, access premium-quality supplies, and build lasting relationships within the sport. This network not only fosters personal growth but also strengthens the global pigeon racing community.

The templates for record-keeping and the step-by-step guides for advanced practices offer practical tools to refine your methods and ensure precision in every aspect of the sport. Whether it's tracking health metrics, analyzing race performance, or managing breeding programs, these resources empower you to approach pigeon racing with a professional and data-driven mindset.

Racing Pigeons Mastery Unleashed

As pigeon racing continues to evolve, the incorporation of technology, sustainability practices, and ethical standards will play an increasingly vital role. From using artificial intelligence in breeding programs to adopting environmentally conscious loft management, the future of the sport lies in innovation and responsibility.

Above all, pigeon racing is more than just a competition—it's a celebration of the bond between humans and birds, built on trust, care, and a shared pursuit of excellence. Whether you aspire to be a world champion, a respected breeder, or a dedicated enthusiast, the journey is as rewarding as the achievements. By applying the knowledge and insights from this book, you are not only honoring the legacy of pigeon racing but also contributing to its vibrant and promising future.

Thank you for embarking on this journey through the art, science, and passion of pigeon racing. May your lofts be thriving, your pigeons soar with unparalleled skill, and your racing endeavors bring you lasting success and joy.